Environmental Impact Assessment Handbook

Environmental Impact Assessment Handbook

A practical guide for planners, developers and communities

Barbara Carroll and Trevor Turpin

Thomas Telford

Published by Thomas Telford Publishing, Thomas Telford Ltd, 1 Heron Quay,
London E14 4JD. URL:
http://www.thomastelford.com

Distributors for Thomas Telford books are
USA: ASCE Press, 1801 Alexander Bell Drive, Reston, VA 20191-4400, USA
Japan: Maruzen Co. Ltd, Book Department, 3-10 Nihonbashi 2-chome, Chuo-ku,
Tokyo 103
Australia: DA Books and Journals, 648 Whitehorse Road, Mitcham 3132, Victoria

First published 2002

Reprinted 2003

Also available from Thomas Telford Books
Planning and environmental protection. An introductory guide. RTPI, 2002.
ISBN 0 7277 3102 5.
Hidden aspects of urban planning. Surface and underground development. T. Paul, F. Chow
and O. Kjekstad (eds), 2002. ISBN 0 7277 3101 7.
Environmental impact assessment. A guide to procedures. DETR, 2000. ISBN 0 7277 2960 8.

A catalogue record for this book is available from the British Library

ISBN: 0 7277 2781 8

© Barbara Carroll and Trevor Turpin, 2002

Printed and bound in Great Britain by Hobbs the Printers, Hampshire

Contents

Preface

Since its birth in the United States just over 30 years ago, a huge literature on environmental impact assessment (EIA), both within the UK and the rest of the world, has been spawned. As one who has contributed his fair share to this, I can confidently say that this Practical Handbook is unique. It is not academic, as so much of the literature tends to be (*mea culpa*), and yet it is likely to prove very useful not only to students, but also to academics seeking to familiarize themselves with a new field. It is not procedural, and yet it explains how the EIA process works and refers the reader gently to the appropriate chapter and verse. It is not theoretical but it describes many of the approaches and methods used in EIA. It is not an activist's charter and yet it provides the ammunition to challenge an environmental statement. Rather, it is an approachable and practical handbook, with numerous illustrated explanations and examples, written from the practitioner's perspective.

Over the dozen or so years we have had EIA in the UK, it has become part of our everyday life. It is increasingly common to hear on the news that the results of an EIA have revealed that some impact or other is likely to be problematic or that protesters have demanded an EIA before a development is allowed to proceed. The concept of environmental assessment is expanding from the evaluation of projects to the environmental appraisal of plans and policies. We all need an accessible, practical explanation of EIA, whether we are developers, consultants, central or local authority officers, environmental regulators, environmental activists, local residents, students or academics. This Practical Handbook is it!

Professor Christopher Wood
EIA Centre
School of Planning and Landscape
University of Manchester

Acknowledgements

In a book of this nature, based as it is on practical experience, gratitude is owed to a wide range of people whose approach and decisions have guided EIAs in particular directions. These include clients, developers, planning authority officers, regulators – especially the Environment Agency and English Nature – and colleagues. To all of them we would like to express our thanks for contributing to what is after all a rapidly developing field … we are all still learning.

We do, however, want to acknowledge specific help from the following individuals:

- Adam Boyden for drafting the sections on transport and soils.
- Alison Fell for drafting the sections on air and noise.

The following have also reviewed particular sections:

Hugh Barton (transport), Andrew Brookes (water), John Hawkes and Peter Cox (heritage), Duncan Laxen (air), Sara Metcalfe (landscape), Roger Prescott (planning and population), Chris Stapleton (soils), David Trevor-Jones (noise), Mike Wells (biodiversity) – for which we are grateful. In all cases, however, errors and omissions remain the responsibility of the authors.

Thanks are due to Sharon Parfitt who developed the authors' design concept, Jane Antrobus, to Linda for the sustaining goodies and to Amanda who is, as ever, a star.

Finally, we must thank our commissioning editor, Maria Stewart of Thomas Telford Publishing, for her patience and persistence.

All photographs and illustrations are either those of the authors or from the libraries of Nicholas Pearson Associates and Enfusion, for which permission to publish is gratefully acknowledged. Exceptions are where otherwise noted and those on the front cover which has been kindly provided by the Bath Spa Project, the photomontage on page 116 which was produced by Nicholas Pearson Associates and is reproduced by permission of Watts Blake and Bearne and BP Exploration for use of the photographs on pages 33 and 117.

Foreword: about this Practical Handbook

The aim of this handbook is to provide practical guidance to the practice of Environmental Impact Assessment (EIA). EIA is a systematic procedure for ensuring that the likely effects of new development on the environment are taken into account in deciding whether the proposed project should go ahead or not. EIA is explained here in accordance with the requirements and format of the UK EIA Regulations (1999). The process of assessing effects on the environment is EIA and the document produced as a result of the assessment is an Environmental Statement (ES).

This guidance is written for planners, designers and developers who need sufficient introduction to EIA to know what needs to be prepared by whom and by when. It will be useful for development project managers as well as students and community groups. The handbook approach has been designed with cross-referencing and checklists which also makes the guide readily useful for easy reference to the EIA practitioner and environmental specialist.

The Objectives of this EIA Handbook

- To present the requirements of EIA according to the UK EIA Regulations in a readily usable and practical way.
- To inspire and share experience towards good EIA practice by a practical handbook format illustrated with case studies.
- To inform and guide the use of EIA early and effectively in the development design and land use planning processes.
- To demonstrate the advantages of improvements in EIA practice to facilitate better informed planning decisions.

Who this EIA Handbook is written for

- Planners of local authorities who need to advise on the requirements for EIA and receive planning applications accompanied by environmental statements (ESs). It will also be useful for other officers dealing with conservation, transport and environmental health issues who will be consulted on such planning applications.

- Professionals regulating projects subject to legislation other than land use planning.

- Developers who need to understand EIA prior to early discussions with local authorities and appointment of specialist consultants.

- Designers, Architects, Engineers, Surveyors, Planners and other professionals working as project managers on development proposals who need to understand why, when and how to include EIA into their projects. The Handbook is also useful to specialists as an easy reference and to understand the requirements of other specialisms and the context within the planning process.

- The statutory consultees in the EIA and land-use planning processes who need to understand their role.

- The community sector who could make use of this guide to assist their understanding of, and participation in, EIA and the development planning process.

- Students of specialist environmental planning courses as well as those students on, e.g. engineering, architecture, planning and related courses who are required to study EIA as a core or subsidiary subject.

- The handbook is written primarily for users in the UK, however, the principles and practice have world-wide applications.

> *Legislation and guidance is generally given for England. The relevant legislation and guidance for Wales, Scotland, Northern Ireland or other countries should always be consulted.*

How this EIA Handbook is structured

The handbook is structured in five chapters. Each chapter is organized in a similar way such that elements, including case studies, key facts, checklists, and sources of further information, have the same layout for easy reference. It is designed to be dipped into but also follows a systematic approach which takes the reader through the EIA process step by step. There is extensive cross-referencing and signposting since EIA is an iterative and multi-disciplinary team process and environmental effects are often inter-related.

Chapter 1: Introduction

An overview of the EIA process, explaining why and when it is necessary to carry out an EIA. The role of EIA within the planning and development processes is introduced, together with standards and the role of environmental management. EIA is placed within the context of sustainable development and links are shown with other mechanisms and consenting procedures in the planning and environmental protection systems.

Chapter 2: Procedures

The roles of an Environmental Impact Assessment (EIA) team, consenting authorities and consultees, together with the legislative and policy context are introduced. The procedures of screening, scoping and consultation are explained. The assessment procedure is outlined with baseline studies, impact assessment and significance, mitigation options, alternatives and monitoring. The process of preparing the Environmental Statement (ES) is summarized and a format for the document is suggested. Post-ES submission procedures are outlined.

Chapter 3: Environmental Topics

Each element of the environment likely to be affected by development is considered in a similar way: responsibilities, standards and legislation, the methodology including baseline studies, potential effects, assessment and significance of impacts, mitigation, further guidance and information. Each section is designed to be self-contained. The environmental topics are listed as presented in the Regulations. Interactions between topics and sustainability are drawn together in the final section.

Chapter 4: Development Types

EIA is site-specific and the extent of potential impacts is dependent on the quality and characteristics of the receiving environment. However, development types tend to have characteristics also and these may suggest typical environmental impacts. This chapter is presented in checklist format for easy reference and lists key potential impacts, mitigation, monitoring, environmental management and further guidance for a range of development types. It also draws attention to the opportunities for environmental enhancement from development proposals.

Chapter 5: Environmental Management

Environmental management reduces the risk of pollution to the environment and improves the sustainable management of environmental resources. This chapter introduces the role of environmental management in EIA and explains how commitments to mitigation and environmental protection can be made in a systematic and transparent way.

How to use this Practical Handbook

Inspiration and insight
quotes and facts

Case example
to illustrate good
(or bad) practice

Section

> In each case, it will be necessary to judge whether the likely effects on the environment of that particular development will be significant in that particular location
> - DETR Circular 02/99

'Sensitive areas' may be designated areas (or others) that may be affected by projects having regard to:

- existing land use
- relative abundance, quality and regenerative capacity of natural resources
- the absorption capacity of the natural environment.

It is impossible to be prescriptive about any particular development and all should be judged on a case-by-case basis. This screening process will need to be applied – as will the views of consultees. Just because a Schedule 2 development project falls within a 'sensitive area' does not automatically mean that EIA will be required. However, sensitive areas do not have to be 'designated' – a congested urban area can be just as sensitive to additional development as an Area of Outstanding Natural Beauty (AONB).

Regulators should also consider cumulative effects of other proposed development and indirect effects of projects.

Screening Opinion

Developers can undertake the screening process themselves or can seek the views and help of the planning authority on whether EIA is needed in a particular case.

To obtain a formal 'screening opinion' from the planning authority in accordance with the Regulations, the developer needs to submit:

- location plan
- brief description of the nature and purpose of the project
- possible scale of environmental effects
- other representations.

It has to be remembered that the planning authority may (although not under an obligation to) seek advice from the statutory or non-statutory consultees at this stage – and the planning authority may be influenced by public response in reaching its decision, even though any opposition should not affect such an opinion. The planning authority has to provide its screening opinion within 3 weeks of receiving a request (or longer if agreed with the developer).

The screening opinion should include aspects of the development's environmental effects which the planning authority considers significant and it has to be made available for public inspection (together with the developer's request).

The Secretary of State may also be asked for a 'screening direction' if the

- developer disagrees with the planning authority's opinion
- planning authority fails to provide an opinion within 3 weeks.

The Secretary of State has to give a screening direction within 3 weeks or such longer period as may be required. This direction will also be made available for public inspection.

case example

Bath Spa Project
A new Spa facility was proposed to provide treatment in the Georgian heart of the World Heritage City of Bath. It was considered that EIA was not required, since, although clearly a sensitive area, the project would not have a significant effect on the environment. (An environmental report was prepared to accompany the planning application.)

Checklists
basic information
presented in
bullet point form

Key fact
Both the planning authority's screening opinion and the developer's request have to be made available for public inspection

Since such opinions are not confidential, details of the project will appear in the public domain at this stage and developers are advised to manage the release of project details prior to this.

There are other circumstances where an EIA is deemed to have been required, where:

- the planning authority (or authorizing body) has given an opinion without a formal screening request that the project is to be subject to EIA and an ES prepared, and this view is not challenged or a ruling is not requested from the Secretary of State
- the promoter volunteers an ES which states that it is an "ES in accordance with the Regulations" and the planning authority accepts the ES
- the promoter and the planning authority (or authorizing body) informally agree that an ES should be prepared.

2.4 Scoping

Definition

Scoping is the way in which key issues are identified from a broad range of potential concerns for inclusion in EIA studies, the areas affected, and the level to which they should be studied. The importance of effective and accurate scoping cannot be over-emphasized.

Legislation

Schedule 4 of the EIA Regulations requires a description of those aspects of the environment likely to be significantly affected *including* population, fauna, flora, soil, water, air, climatic factors, material assets (including the architectural and archaeological heritage), landscape and the inter-relationship between them.

Discussion

The EIA guide to the procedures (DETR 2000) includes the above checklist of matters to be considered; it is unlikely that all will be relevant to any one project. Being at the beginning of the EIA process it is fundamental to get scoping right: studies of the quality of ESs have frequently blamed inadequacies on poor or inadequate scoping. Government advice is that the relevant authorities and the statutory consultees should be involved from an early stage before the preparation of the ES.

Many consultees, faced with an EIA development for the first time, and asked which issues should be addressed will reproduce the EC Directive, the Regulations, or both.

EIAs are carried out usually under time, budget and resource constraints. Spending time on a non-issue will result in less for the important matters and potentially non-determination for lack of information. This is frustrating

case example

Britannia Ironworks
Despite being allocated in the local plan for housing, the Secretary of State directed that, due to contamination from previous industrial uses, an application for redevelopment of the site, even in outline, required an Environmental Statement.

Further information

Further information
Guidance on Scoping 2001 Europa.Eu.int
Environment Agency 1996 Scoping Handbook

Key fact
Schedule 4 of the Regulations lists elements of the environment which might be affected – it does not require them all to be addressed

guiding principle

Early and effective scoping results in effective use of resources and time

Guiding principles

Abbreviations

ALC	Agricultural Land Classification
AONB	Area of Outstanding Natural Beauty
AST	Appraisal Summary Table
BAP	Biodiversity Action Plan
BAT	Best Available Techniques
BGS	British Geological Survey
BMA	British Medical Association
BMWP	Biological Monitoring Working Party
BOD	Biochemical Oxygen Demand
BREEAM	The Building Research Establishment Environmental Assessment Method
BS	British Standard
CABE	Commission for Architecture and the Built Environment
CAMS	Catchment Abstraction Management Strategies
CCW	Countryside Council for Wales
CEA	Cumulative Effects Assessment
CHaMP	Coastal Habitat Management Plan
CIEH	Chartered Institute of Environmental Health
CIRIA	Construction Industry Research and Information Association
CITES	Convention on International Trade in Endangered Species
CIWEM	Chartered Institution of Water and Environmental Management
CInstWM	Chartered Institute of Wastes Management
COMAH	Control of Major Accident Hazards
COSHH	Control of Substances Hazardous to Health
CPRE	Council for the Protection of Rural England
CRTN	Calculation of Road Traffic Noise
CZM	Coastal Zone Management
dB_A	Decibels (A-weighted)
DETR	Department of Environment, Transport and the Regions
DEFRA	Department for Environment, Food and Rural Affairs
DIS	Draft International Standard
DMRB	Design Manual for Roads and Bridges
DOE	Department of Environment
DoE NI	Department of the Environment, Northern Ireland
DOH	Department of Health
DTI	Department of Trade and Industry
DTLR	Department of Transport, Local Government and the Regions
EA	Environment Agency
EC	European Commission
EHIA	Environmental Health Impact Assessment
EHO	Environmental Health Officer
EIA	Environmental Impact Assessment
ES	Environmental Statement
EMP	Environmental Management Plan
EMS	Environmental Management System
EQS	Environmental Quality Standard
ESA	Environmentally Sensitive Area

ETSU	Energy Technology Support Unit
EU	European Union
FRCA	Farming and Rural Conservation Agency
GDPO	General Development Procedure Order
GPDO	General Permitted Development Order
GOMMMS	Guidance on the Methodology for Multi-Modal Studies
HAP	Habitat Action Plan
HBF	House Builders Federation
HDV	Heavy Duty Vehicle
HGV	Heavy Goods Vehicle
HIA	Health Impact Assessment
Hz	Hertz
IAIA	International Association for Impact Assessment
ICRCL	Inter-Departmental Committee on the Redevelopment of Contaminated Land
IDB	Internal Drainage Board
IEEM	Institute of Ecology and Environmental Management
IEMA	Institute of Environmental Management and Assessment
IFA	Institute of Field Archaeologists
IHT	Institution of Highways and Transportation
IPPC	Integrated Pollution Prevention and Control
ISO	International Organization for Standardization
IUCN	International Union for the Conservation of Nature
JNCC	Joint Nature Conservancy Council
LAPPC	Local Air Pollution Prevention and Control
LAQM	Local Air Quality Management
LEAP	Local Environment Agency Plan
LPA	Local Planning Authority
LTP	Local Transport Plan
MAFF	Ministry of Agriculture, Fisheries and Food
NATA	New Approach to Appraisal
NSCA	National Society for Clean Air
NTS	Non-Technical Summary
NVC	National Vegetation Classification
OS	Ordnance Survey
pe	population equivalent
PM_{10}	Particulates
PPC	Pollution Prevention and Control
PPG	Planning Policy Guidance
QoL	Quality of Life
RBD	River Basin District
RBMP	River Basin Management Plan
RCEP	Royal Commission on Environmental Pollution
RIGS	Regionally Important Geological Site
RIVPACS	River Invertebrate Prediction and Classification System
ROMP	Review of Minerals Permissions
RSPB	Royal Society for the Protection of Birds
RTPI	Royal Town Planning Institute
SA	Sustainability Appraisal
SAC	Special Area of Conservation
SAM	Scheduled Ancient Monument
SAP	Species Action Plan
SD	Sustainable Development
SEA	Strategic Environmental Assessment
SEPA	Scottish Environmental Protection Agency
SI	Système International d'Unites

SIA	Social Impact Assessment
SINC	Site of Importance for Nature Conservation
SMR	Sites and Monuments Record
SMP	Shoreline Management Plan
SNH	Scottish Natural Heritage
SPA	Special Protection Area
SPAB	Society for the Protection of Ancient Buildings
SPZ	Special Protection Zone
SSSI	Site of Special Scientific Interest
SUDS	Sustainable Urban Drainage System
TA	Transport Assessment
TCPA	Town and Country Planning Association
TIA	Traffic Impact Assessment
TRICS	Trip Rate Information Computer System
TRL	Transport Research Laboratory
UK	United Kingdom
UN	United Nations
UNESCO	United Nations Educational, Scientific and Cultural Organization
VEC	Valued Ecosystem Component
WHO	World Health Organization
WIA	Water Industry Act
WLMP	Water Level Management Plan
WRA	Water Resources Act
ZVI	Zone of Visual Influence

Chapter 1

Introduction

'Consult the Genius of the Place in all ...'

Alexander Pope 1731

An overview of the EIA process, explaining why and when it is necessary to carry out an EIA. The role of EIA within the planning and development processes is introduced, together with standards and the role of environmental management. EIA is placed within the context of sustainable development and links are shown with other mechanisms and consenting procedures in the planning and environmental protection systems.

Contents

EIA is an important procedure for ensuring that the likely effects of new development on the environment are fully understood and taken into account before the development is allowed to go ahead

– DETR 2000, EIA A Guide to Procedures

Key fact

Environmental issues are not necessarily a constraint on development: environmental enhancement can facilitate sustainable development

1.1   What is Environmental Impact Assessment?

Environment Impact Assessment (EIA) is a procedure which serves to provide information to local authority planners, other regulators and authorizing bodies, other interested parties and the general public, about certain proposed developments and their likely effects on the environment. It also enables developers, on whose behalf the EIA is generally undertaken, to meet their own environmental standards, to minimize environmental impacts and facilitate the approval process. It is a technique which has developed over the past 30 years and is applied by governments and international institutions throughout the world.

It must be emphasized that EIA is **part** of the process of deciding whether certain types of development projects should be approved. Other dimensions – political, local feelings and cultures, overriding need, competing proposals – also have to be considered. However, by including environmental factors **alongside** social and economic considerations, a more sustainable approach to development is ensured.

EIA is the **whole process** the collection and assessment of information **and** the determination of the application for development approval. It is undertaken by, or on behalf of, a developer or investor. Nonetheless, early and continued positive dialogue is encouraged between the promoter, the authorizing body, other consultees and the public. The process identifies the potential significant effects on the environment and develops appropriate options for their mitigation.

1.2 Some Definitions

Environmental Impact Assessment (EIA): the process assessing the environmental impacts of development projects.

Environmental Statement (ES): the document reporting the EIA.

Mitigation: avoiding, reducing or remedying potential adverse impacts.

Compensation: replacing an adverse impact either in kind or something of a different nature to that which may be lost.

Enhancement: improving elements of the environment.

Screening: the process to decide if EIA is required.

Scoping: the process to identify the key environmental issues.

Consultees: statutory and non-statutory interested parties.

Strategic Environmental Assessment (SEA): environmental assessment of plans and programmes.

1.3 The Need for EIA

The need for EIA is derived from the EU Directive on the assessment of certain public and private projects on the environment, first introduced in 1985 and amended in 1997. It was incorporated into UK legislation in 1988 and the current Regulations date from 1999.

EIA applies to major developments for which planning approval is required from local authorities under the Town and Country Planning Act 1990, and also to many projects which are outside the planning system and require authorization from other bodies:

- trunk roads and motorways
- power stations, overhead power lines and long distance oil and gas pipelines
- afforestation
- land drainage improvements – (including flood and coastal defence)
- ports and harbours
- marine fish farming
- marine dredging for minerals
- projects under the Transport and Works Act 1992 (e.g. railways, inland waterways).

Major projects for which EIA may be required are listed in the Directive and the Regulations. They are divided into Schedule 1 and Schedule 2 developments. Schedule 1 projects, e.g. nuclear power stations, always require EIA. Schedule 2 projects are those listed in the Regulations and where EIA will only be required if significant environmental effects are likely to arise. Criteria and thresholds for significance are set out in the DETR Circular 02/99 and are reproduced in Appendix 2 of this handbook. The key word is **significant** and the Circular suggests three main criteria of significance:

- major developments
- environmentally sensitive locations
- complex developments with hazardous effects.

Key legislation and guidance

EU Directive 85/387/EEC as amended by 97/11/EC The assessment of effects of certain public and private projects on the environment

Town & Country (EIA) (England and Wales) Regulations 1999

DETR 1999 Circular 02/99 Environmental Impact Assessment

DETR 2000 EIA A Guide to Procedures

www.dtlr.gov.uk

EU EIA studies, reports and guidance www.europa.eu.int

EU Directive 2001/42/EC Strategic Environmental Assessment

UN Environment Programme studies, reports and guidance www.unep.org

www.worldbank.org

Key fact

The UK Government proposes to dispense with public inquiries for major controversial projects and rely on parliamentary and ministerial approval

Key fact

Planning is concerned with

- creating opportunities for development
- conserving environmental quality
- achieving sustainable development
- promoting public participation
- protecting the rights of the individual

– DTLR 2001

The legislation allows for guidance on whether an EIA is necessary for Schedule 2 projects from the local authority and the Secretary of State. Developers can apply to the competent authority for a *'screening opinion'* on whether EIA is needed.

Permitted Development Rights (PDRs): Schedule 1 projects are not permitted development and always require submission of a planning application and an ES. PDRs for Schedule 2 projects are also withdrawn unless the planning authority has given a screening opinion that EIA is not required. Special considerations apply to projects proposed for simplified planning and enterprise zones.

1.4   The Purpose of EIA

Environmental Protection: The EC directive was promoted by the Trade Department of the European Commission, and the underlying reason was to ensure that a level playing field prevailed in the competitive conditions of a common market. However the stated aim, and the one which is often overlooked, is in the Preamble to the 1985 Directive:

'...the best environmental policy consists in preventing the creation of pollution or nuisances at sources, rather than subsequently trying to counteract their effects; ... [and] to take effects on the environment into account at the earliest possible stage in all the technical planning and decision-making processes; ...'

So, EIA is actually about the reduction or minimization of pollution in its widest sense. While EIA is part of the planning system in the UK, separate approvals may also be required for certain developments, e.g. Pollution Prevention and Control (PPC), land drainage and discharge consents. Planning authorities look to other agencies to confirm compliance or satisfactory standards; Planning Policy Guidance (PPG) 23 Planning and Pollution Control encourages approval procedures to run simultaneously and to avoid duplication of controls.

Design and Planning: The integration of the emerging design of a development into the EIA process can ensure that a proposal with the least damaging environmental effects is arrived at. This can facilitate consideration of alternative approaches to development and lead to a more robust planning application. By taking account at the earliest possible stage of such issues as the design of the development, the process, location and site, the design can be influenced such that major changes or onerous planning conditions are not required too late in the project programme.

The presentation of the environmental information in a transparent and systematic way assists the competent authorities when determining the application for approval. This can also allay the general public's concerns which are often based on the fear of unknown effects.

Management: EIA can also be used as a management tool by contributing to environmental risk assessment, identifying hazards at the design stage and presenting the opportunity to design them out and ensuring that risks are managed throughout the project.

The commitment to environmental management which is made in the ES can be conditioned by regulators and incorporated into contract documents, thus ensuring continued protection of the environment from construction through to final restoration.

Further information

Town and Country Planning (General Permitted Development) Order 1995

Key legislation and guidance

PPC Regulations 2000

PPG 23 Planning and Pollution Control

Key facts

The EIA Regulations require consideration of *'the regenerative capacity of natural resources [and] the absorptive capacity of the natural environment.'*

The government's commitment to good design is presented in PPG 1 and confirmed in PPG 3 which requires local authorities and housebuilders to design for quality

"
An ES provides a useful framework within which environmental considerations and design development can interact

– DETR 2000
"

Further information

PPG 1 General Policy and Principles

PPG 3 Housing

DETR 2000 Urban design in the planning system: towards better practice

Urban Design Alliance

Commission for Architecture and the Built Environment (CABE)

1.5 The Process of EIA

Those environmental issues which may be significant in the context of the proposed development are identified by the scoping exercise. Provision is made in the Regulations for formal scoping by consultation with interested parties. The EIA process then comprises review of existing information through desk studies and site surveys. For each significant environmental issue, baseline conditions are identified and the likely effects of the development are then predicted. The magnitude and significance of the effects – including indirect and cumulative – are then assessed. Mitigation measures are incorporated throughout the iterative process of design and EIA in order to achieve a 'no net loss' to the environment. This requires team effort and interactions both within the development team itself and with the external contributors.

Consultation is inherent in the EIA process and is continuous throughout, involving statutory and non-statutory consultees as well as the public; it feeds into the evolving design in an interactive way. Early and thorough consultation will identify those interested parties who might be concerned about the proposed development.

The Regulations and the Directive indicate what should be included within an ES:

- description of the site and development
- outline of main alternatives studied
- significant direct and indirect effects
- measures to prevent, reduce or offset significant adverse effects
- non-technical summary (NTS).

An important requirement is an NTS and this confirms that the approach of EIA has to be understandable by planning professionals, elected members and the general public. The ES itself should, therefore, reflect this.

The EIA process continues through to determination; approval may be made with conditions. These can require monitoring and management of the development, carrying the commitments made in the ES through the construction and occupation stages. The ES should include a section on environmental management identifying mitigation measures and the specification of the means of their implementation.

1.6 Professional Standards and Review

The ES will be reviewed by the competent authority (either internally or by consultants). The ES review will look at the adequacy of information and may entail consulting with other agencies. There are review systems available which systematically check the adequacy of the ES against the legislative requirements. The Institute of Environmental Management and Assessment (IEMA), formerly the Institute of Environmental Assessment, was established to improve the standard of ESs (Wood and Jones reported on the inadequacy of the majority of ESs in the 1980s) and, more recently, the adequacy of ESs has been challenged through Judicial Review. IEMA has established criteria based on the work of the EIA Centre at the University of Manchester. Many planning authorities will

Key fact

Sufficient information to assess the environmental effects must be provided for both outline and detailed planning applications

Key fact

In the UK planning system, consideration of a planning application is subject to an 8-week determination period – for applications with an ES, 16 weeks is allowed for the decision-making process

Key fact

The modernization of the UK planning system is placing more emphasis on public participation

Further information

DoE 1995 Preparation of Environmental Statements: A Good Practice Guide

DTLR 2001 Planning: delivering a fundamental change

seek advice from IEMA because of their own inexperience of such major developments or lack of resources.

IEMA is the professional institute for EIA and other institutions maintain professional standards for other disciplines which contribute to EIA.

1.7   Links

Strategic Environmental Assessment (SEA) considers the environmental effects of plans and programmes and is the process that the EC originally proposed prior to project EIA. The long overdue Directive on SEA was published in 2001 and has to be implemented into the legislation of Member States by 2004. Methodologies for Sustainability Appraisal (SA) have been developed to appraise the sustainability of development plans in the UK (and as required by PPG 12 Development Plans). These have tended to evolve from SEA methods and include the social and economic elements of the agenda as well as environmental.

Sustainable Development (SD) is now enshrined in the UK planning system and EIA is a technique which can assist in progressing the objectives and principles of sustainable development by protecting natural resources and the environment. The relationships between the wider environment and health/social well-being are increasingly being understood. Similarly, the opportunities to facilitate development and regeneration through improved environmental conditions are becoming recognized. Sustainability of resource usage in design and construction, including energy and materials should, therefore, be reported in the ES.

The commitment to mitigation reported in an ES through a draft Environmental Management Plan (EMP) can provide the framework for the regulators and the contractors. If the developer and/or the contractor have an Environmental Management System (EMS), additional reassurance will be given to regulators and public. The new international standard ISO/DIS 19011 will help organizations integrate quality and environmental management allowing a single audit of both systems.

1.8   The Future

This handbook aims to be a pragmatic guide for everyone involved in the EIA process and to ensure that legal requirements are met. However, legislation and practice continually change and, therefore, we guide the reader in the direction of good practice, where appropriate, and with an awareness of emerging issues and requirements. For example, the Human Rights Act 1998 has been shown to test claims made in ESs and planning authorities will have to consider whether their decisions have an impact on the rights of the individual. The ES will be a critical tool in this respect.

'The EIA process as a primary instrument for development planning and decision-making, can serve as a crucial action-forcing mechanism for sustainable development...there will be considerable scope for the creative application of impact compensation ... via resource conservation, rehabilitation or enhancement measures ...'

Sadler 1999

IEMA
- Professional standards
- Research and opinions
- ES reviews

The Centre for Environmental Assessment and Management (CEAM) at the Institute undertakes research in the field of EIA, produces Guidelines on particular topics and delivers services to IEMA corporate members.

www.iema.net

Objectives of Sustainable Development
- Maintenance of high and stable economic growth and employment
- Social progress which recognizes the needs of everyone
- Effective protection of the environment
- Prudent use of natural resources
– DETR 1999 The UK Sustainable Development Strategy

"
we are all environmental managers now

Environment Agency 2000
An Environmental Vision   "

Further information

DETR 1999 The UK Sustainable Development Strategy

DETR 1999 Proposals for a Good Practice Guide on Sustainability Appraisal of Regional Planning Guidance

RSPB/Bedfordshire County Council 1996 Step by Step Guide to Environmental Appraisal

PPG 12 Development Plans

DETR 2000 A Strategy for more sustainable construction

"
In the beginning we built cities to overcome our environment. In the future we must build cities to nurture it

– Sir Richard Rogers Reith Lectures 1995   "

Greenwich Millennium Village and Ecology Park

Chapter 2

Procedures

The roles of an Environmental Impact Assessment (EIA) team, consenting author-ities and consultees, together with the legislative and policy context are intro-duced. The procedures of screening, scoping and consultation are explained. The assessment procedure is outlined with baseline studies, impact assessment and significance, mitigation options, alternatives and monitoring. The process of preparing the Environmental Statement (ES) is summarized and a format for the document is suggested. Post-ES submission procedures are outlined.

2.1   Introduction

This chapter focuses on what is required and expected of a team under-taking an EIA of a development proposal. In this sense, it is very much concerned with **development** and how that will need to fit in with:

- concepts and principles of sustainability
- plans, policies and programmes of local authorities, central and regional government and guidance notes
- policies of other organizations, e.g. the Environment Agency (EA).

The word 'team' is deliberate: the 1999 EIA Regulations encourage active dialogue between the developer and the authority who will ultimately receive the ES, far more than the previous Regulations. It is no longer nec-essarily left entirely to the developer to decide – however skilfully, profes-sionally and impartially – which topics to address and to what level of detail. Such an active role by planning authorities will be welcomed by many who have encountered difficulties with indecision, prevarication or inexperience in the past.

It is recognized that inexperience will remain – there are some 480 plan-ning authorities in the UK and, given an average of 300 ESs per year – inevitably usually focused on areas where development is encouraged or profitable – then there will be some authorities who are rarely involved in EIA. However, this is no excuse or reason for inaction or indecision. Planning authorities are required, *if asked*, to give both Screening and Scoping Opinions and if they do not feel competent to give such opinions they can readily enlist the support of other bodies or consultancies: many authorities use the services of the Institute of Environmental Management and Assessment (IEMA), who are also producing EIA process guidelines.

There has been provision since the implementation of the EC Directive into the UK EIA Regulations in 1988, for obtaining the opinions of either local authorities or the Secretary of State as to whether EIA is required. Some commentators have noted that this opinion is rarely sought or chal-lenged. In practical terms, however, this is perhaps not surprising: the pri-mary objective of a developer is almost invariably to secure consent for development, not to avoid an EIA and ES. It has always been readily apparent if proposed development falls within the scope of the EIA

Contents

"

EIA provides a basis for better decision making

– DETR 2000, EIA A Guide to Procedures   "

case example

Even in 2000, one local planning authority asked for an extension of time to provide a Scoping Opinion and eventually sent a photocopy of a section of the Regulations. The legislation expects a more sophisticated response!

Further information

www.dtlr.gov.uk/planning

www.iema.net

www.europa.eu.int

info@iaia.org

Regulations; the 1999 Regulations and Circular 02/99 provide even more guidance in terms of specific thresholds for when an EIA is required or not.

The main steps in the EIA process are outlined in the following diagram, which makes it clear that consultation is an integral part of the process. On receipt of the ES, the determining authority will review it for content and completeness and (in the case of a planning authority), the officer's report on the application, based on responses from consultees, will be considered by committee usually within 16 weeks of receipt of the ES.

Outline of EIA Process

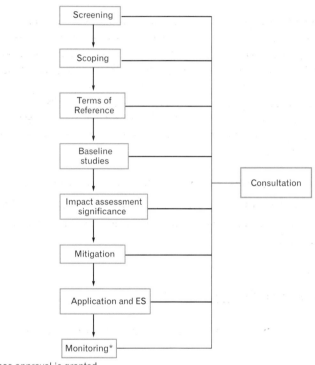

*assumes approval is granted.

2.2 Getting Started

The Development Project and EIA Inception

The need for EIA will be decided, although frequently not immediately recognized, at the stage when a development requiring planning consent (or other authorizations) is proposed. For example, such development may be part of an energy company's programme in exploitation of new resources, a government department's road building programme, the EA's flood protection programme, or landowners seeking to create a new settlement. For a continuing development programme, contact will already have been made with the relevant planning authority or equivalent. For a new development, early consultation with that body will be required. The authority should be mindful of the potential need for EIA and should advise the applicants as early as possible.

Where alternatives to the proposed development are likely to be discussed in the EIA, i.e. location, process or construction methodology, their relative merits should be considered and recorded at this early stage – in a systematic and thorough manner using criteria to gauge the relative environmental impact of alternatives considered. Scheme promoters will have a development team including a project manager, legal representation, surveyors, planners, architects and engineers. At this stage, it must be established whether the need for EIA falls within the planning system or other regulatory controls. At the point where the potential need for EIA is required, an EIA specialist should be appointed.

Key fact

EIA assessors registered with IEMA have to satisfy necessary skills and experience criteria.

Guidelines for registration: www.iema.net

The Project Team

The EIA element of a proposed development requires a project manager. Various professions have claimed that they are best suited to lead EIA studies, including planners because EIA is usually part of the planning process and architects because EIA runs parallel to and should be integrated with the design process. In order to lead a successful approach to EIA, negotiation at all stages of the process will be required combined with skills to co-ordinate with the development team and specialists. There are several approaches, any of which may work dependent on the circumstances, including:

- client appoints EIA team leader from within own organization
- consultancy appointed to undertake design or planning, and EIA
- EIA specialist appointed to co-ordinate EIA and administer tendering process for specialist tasks.

Project Terms of Reference

Prior to *'going public'* on any development proposal, the following should be determined:

- development mix and objectives
- budget for planning and development costs
- programme for approval
- timescale for development
- options for alternatives (locations/processes)
- budget for construction, operation and restoration (if appropriate).

Ranges for these parameters should be decided by the development team together with any options for flexibility before consultation starts. If members of the team are not aware of flexibility or potential cost limitations, the consultation process will not be as beneficial as it could be. These issues have to be decided by the project team.

Communication and Initial Consultation

What is often neglected is the provision of advice on how the project is likely to be perceived by the receiving public. Therefore, public relations

Key fact

Lack of information leads to fear of the unknown which can result in opposition

Getting Started

Combe Down Stone Mines

Combe Down Stone Mines are 18th and 19th century shallow mines under the World Heritage City of Bath. Several collapses led to a feasibility study with experimental stabilization techniques including the mobilization of plant on a village green – without advising residents or local councillors. This fear of the unknown provoked the rapid formation of a residents' opposition group and an atmosphere of mistrust which plagued attempts to find a solution. Five years later in 2000, a joint community and council team embarked on a new feasibility study – incorporating EIA

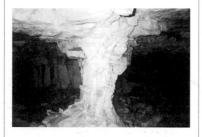

Combe Down Mines: poor condition of underground pillar

advice may be helpful. The role of such specialists is not to put a spin or gloss on the professional EIA process but is to ensure that information is provided in a way that is least likely to alarm the general public. Advice of local planning officers is invaluable in this respect – they know the councillors and they should know what is likely to be required to inform local residents: advice can be provided about the need and timing of local exhibitions to explain the proposals.

If the proposer of the scheme is a multi-national then the advice of a local team member who can effect local introductions can be invaluable – both for the developer and for the planning authority: the last thing they need is a protest group disrupting the planning process. Confrontation between developers and the public – with the determining authority in the middle – is to be avoided and public participation is to be encouraged.

This process has to be managed carefully, yet it is frequently constrained by urgency to submit a planning application and reasons of commercial confidentiality.

While preparatory discussions can be held *'in confidence'*, inevitably news will leak out – news which in the absence of hard facts will frequently be conjecture. The outline of the proposal should, therefore, be presented at an early stage in as much detail as possible and to a rigorous defined programme:

- local authority planners and statutory consultees – in confidence (include adjacent administrative areas)
- local authority members – these are the decision-makers
- local press
- Parish Council presentation
- public exhibition and draft ES where appropriate
- full consultation with statutory and non-statutory groups.

The EIA Regulations require publicity of planning applications accompanied by an ES. However, these legislative requirements should be regarded as the minimum.

EIA good practice has always included early consultation, which then needs to continue as an iterative part of the whole EIA process. The government has made it clear that increased public participation is important in the on-going modernization of the UK planning system.

Key fact

Government is promoting more *public participation* in planning and development decision making, e.g. there is a requirement for local authorities to prepare Community Strategies (DETR 2000) and Local Strategic Partnerships (DETR 2001). An EU Directive has been drafted on public participation

Further guidance

IEMA 2002, Public Consultation Guidelines for EIA

Public consultation has the following aims:

- to explain the nature of the proposal and its potential effects
- to understand the strength and nature of public views of the proposal and to input these into the assessment
- to gather support for the scheme or to reduce opposition by eliminating the fear of the unknown.

Details of preliminary consultation for EIA are given in Section 2.4 and full consultation in Section 2.5.

2.3 Screening

Definition

Screening is the process by which it is decided if an EIA will be required for a proposed development. For this purpose, it has to be determined if a development is described in Schedule 1 or 2 to the Regulations.

Legislation and Discussion

Schedule 1 projects are the major and potentially most polluting developments and always require EIA. Many of these development types have thresholds, e.g. pipelines having a diameter of more than 800 mm and a length of more than 40 km. (Below which they are Schedule 2.)

Key fact

Schedule 1 projects always require EIA

Schedule 2 projects may require EIA depending on size, nature and location *(see Appendix 2)*

Further information

Guidance on screening 2001
www.europa.eu.int

Schedule 1 projects: development types requiring EIA (some have thresholds below which they are Schedule 2)

- Crude oil refineries
- Power stations
- Nuclear fuel reprocessing
- Iron, steel and other metal works
- Asbestos works
- Chemical and other industrial works
- Railways, airports, motorways and new roads
- Waterways and ports
- Waste disposal plants and landfill
- Groundwater abstraction

- Transfer of water resources
- Wastewater treatment plant
- Extraction of petroleum and natural gas
- Dams
- Pipelines
- Intensive pig and poultry rearing
- Industrial pulp, paper and board production
- Quarries and open cast mining
- Storage of petroleum or chemical products

EIA A guide to procedures Appendix 2
DETR 2000

Identifying **Schedule 2 projects** is less straightforward than Schedule 1. Appendix 3 to the EIA guide to the procedures (DETR 2000) sets out the descriptions of development and applicable (and indicative) thresholds and criteria for the purpose of classifying development as Schedule 2; the table is reproduced in Appendix 2 of this handbook, for ease of reference. For example, a proposed wastewater treatment plant treating effluent from more than 150,000 population equivalent (pe) is Schedule 1 and requires an EIA. A smaller plant with more than 100,000 pe but less than 150,000 pe is Schedule 2, and EIA will be required to be formally considered, *if* the area of the development exceeds 1000 m^2 (but not necessarily required).

Schedule 2 projects have to be listed in Schedule 2 and either be in whole or in part in a *'sensitive area'* or meet criteria or exceed certain thresholds. The basic test is the likelihood of significant effects on the environment arising from development and will be assessed (by planning authorities) for projects generally as set out in Schedule 3 of the Regulations.

Provision in Regulations for screening for projects outside of the planning system is varied.

Selection criteria on the need for EIA

- Characteristics of the development
- Location of the development
- Characteristics of the potential impact

Key significance criteria

- of more than local importance
- in particularly sensitive or vulnerable locations
- with potentially complex or hazardous effects

Screening

case example

Bath Spa Project

A new Spa facility was proposed to provide treatment in the Georgian heart of the World Heritage City of Bath. It was considered that EIA was not required, since, although clearly a sensitive area, the project would not have a significant effect on the environment. (An environmental report was prepared to accompany the planning application.)

Key fact

Both the planning authority's screening opinion and the developer's request have to be made available for public inspection

'Sensitive areas' may be designated areas (or others) that may be affected by projects having regard to:

- existing land use
- relative abundance, quality and regenerative capacity of natural resources
- the absorption capacity of the natural environment.

It is impossible to be prescriptive about any particular development and all should be judged on a case-by-case basis. This screening process will need to be applied – as will the views of consultees. Just because a Schedule 2 development project falls within a *'sensitive area'* does not automatically mean that EIA will be required. However, sensitive areas do not have to be 'designated' – a congested urban area can be just as sensitive to additional development as an Area of Outstanding Natural Beauty (AONB).

Regulators should also consider cumulative effects of other proposed development and indirect effects of projects.

Screening Opinion

Developers can undertake the screening process themselves or can seek the views and help of the planning authority on whether EIA is needed in a particular case.

To obtain a formal *'screening opinion'* from the planning authority in accordance with the Regulations, the developer needs to submit:

- location plan
- brief description of the nature and purpose of the project
- possible scale of environmental effects
- other representations.

It has to be remembered that the planning authority may (although not under an obligation to) seek advice from the statutory or non-statutory consultees at this stage – and the planning authority may be influenced by public response in reaching its decision, even though any opposition should not affect such an opinion. The planning authority has to provide its screening opinion within 3 weeks of receiving a request (or longer if agreed with the developer).

The screening opinion should include aspects of the development's environmental effects which the planning authority considers significant and it has to be made available for public inspection (together with the developer's request).

The Secretary of State may also be asked for a *'screening direction'* if the

- developer disagrees with the planning authority's opinion
- planning authority fails to provide an opinion within 3 weeks.

The Secretary of State has to give a screening direction within 3 weeks or such longer period as may be required. This direction will also be made available for public inspection.

Since such opinions are not confidential, details of the project will appear in the public domain at this stage and developers are advised to manage the release of project details prior to this.

There are other circumstances where an EIA is deemed to have been required, where:

- the planning authority (or authorizing body) has given an opinion without a formal screening request that the project is to be subject to EIA and an ES prepared, and this view is not challenged or a ruling is not requested from the Secretary of State
- the promoter volunteers an ES which states that it is an "ES in accordance with the Regulations" and the planning authority accepts the ES
- the promoter and the planning authority (or authorizing body) informally agree that an ES should be prepared.

2.4   Scoping

Definition

Scoping is the way in which key issues are identified from a broad range of potential concerns for inclusion in EIA studies, the areas affected, and the level to which they should be studied. The importance of effective and accurate scoping cannot be over-emphasized.

Legislation

Schedule 4 of the EIA Regulations requires a description of those aspects of the environment likely to be significantly affected *including* population, fauna, flora, soil, water, air, climatic factors, material assets (including the architectural and archaeological heritage), landscape and the inter-relationship between them.

Discussion

The EIA guide to the procedures (DETR 2000) includes the above checklist of matters to be considered; it is unlikely that all will be relevant to any one project. Being at the beginning of the EIA process it is fundamental to get scoping right: studies of the quality of ESs have frequently blamed inadequacies on poor or inadequate scoping. Government advice is that the relevant authorities and the statutory consultees should be involved from an early stage before the preparation of the ES.

Many consultees, faced with an EIA development for the first time, and asked which issues should be addressed will reproduce the EC Directive, the Regulations, or both.

EIAs are carried out usually under time, budget and resource constraints. Spending time on a non-issue will result in less for the important matters and potentially non-determination for lack of information. This is frustrating

case example

Britannia Ironworks

Despite being allocated in the local plan for housing, the Secretary of State directed that, due to contamination from previous industrial uses, an application for redevelopment of the site, even in outline, required an Environmental Statement.

Further information

Guidance on Scoping 2001 Europa.Eu.int
Environment Agency 1996 Scoping Handbook

Key fact

Schedule 4 of the Regulations lists elements of the environment which might be affected – it does not require them all to be addressed

guiding principle

Early and effective scoping results in effective use of resources and time

Scoping

for the developer and time-consuming for the regulators and consultees. Focusing on issues focuses resources.

Impacts which are not addressed nevertheless should be referred to in the ES to show that they were properly considered. Agreement with a regulatory body not to study a particular issue should be recorded. Issues can include not only the topic itself but also consideration of alternative sites or processes where they exist.

Key fact

Scoping sets the Terms of Reference for the EIA

Effective scoping allows the project promoter to assess:

- the appropriateness of the scheme
- the range of issues likely to be raised
- planning and development costs
- programme and timescale to secure determination.

Scoping Opinion

The Regulations make provision for obtaining formal *"scoping opinions"* from the local planning authority (provisions vary with 'non-planning' regulations) or directions from the Secretary of State similar to that for screening as described above.

Formal Scoping Procedure

> Developer writes to planning authority for their scoping opinion (this can be in the form of a Scoping Report) and includes:
> - plan
> - brief description of the nature and purpose of development and its possible effects on the environment
> - other information or representations

↓

> Planning authority requests further information if necessary

↓

Statutory consultees for EIA:

- Relevant local council(s)
- The Countryside Agency*
- English Nature*
- The Environment Agency*
- The statutory consultees under Article 10 of the Town and Country Planning (GDP) Order 1995 for any planning application

And equivalent bodies in Scotland, Wales and Northern Ireland.

> Planning authority consults:
> - the developer
> - statutory and other consultees

↓

> Planning authority considers:
> - characteristics of the particular type of development
> - the environmental features likely to be affected

↓

> Planning authority provides scoping opinion within 5 weeks
> (or longer if agreed)

(The developer *can* request a scoping opinion at the same time as the screening opinion. The planning authority then still has 5 weeks after providing the screening opinion to provide the scoping opinion.)

If an authority fails to provide a scoping opinion within the agreed time, the developer may apply to the Secretary of State; requests should be copied to the planning authority. The Secretary of State can ask for further information from both the developer and the planning authority and will then consult with the developer and the consultation bodies. While the Secretary of State has 5 weeks *'or such longer period as he may reasonably require'* there is no provision to agree a time limit with the applicant.

Even though the planning authority and the Secretary of State may not have asked for additional information in giving their respective scoping opinions, they can ask for it if necessary after submission of the ES.

There is no requirement to seek a formal scoping opinion. However, the Regulations and Circular are very clear that the preparation of the ES should be a collaborative exercise involving discussions with the planning authority, statutory consultees and others. Seeking a scoping opinion can facilitate a useful mechanism for dialogue.

All parties in the EIA process should note that scoping opinions are available for inspection by the general public for up to 2 years at the planning authority's offices.

Requirement for assessment of environmental effects under other legislation

Any assessments of environmental effects required by other legislation should be identified at an early stage of the EIA process. Where more than one requirement applies, unnecessary time and effort is saved if links are identified and the different assessments co-ordinated. Planning Policy Guidance (PPG) 23 gives guidance on the links between the planning process and the pollution control regulatory system; similarly, PPG 9 gives guidance on nature conservation regulatory links.

The Scoping Exercise

While EIA is essentially an iterative process, the scoping exercise begins to define who is likely to be involved in the proposals, what studies are necessary, and to what level of detail they are examined.

Like all activities in the EIA process, all requests and correspondence with consultees should be recorded for incorporation within a Scoping Report which can form part of the ES. The Scoping Report is sent to the planning authority (or authorizing body) with copies to consultees. The typical contents of a Scoping Report are:

- brief description of development and activities
- principal emissions
- sensitivity of receiving environment
- results of initial desk studies and site surveys

Key fact

The Circular 02/99 emphasizes that an ES which does not fully comply with any scoping opinion or direction would not necessarily be invalid but it *'will probably be subject to calls for further information'*

Other EIA links

- Habitats Regulations 1994
- Birds Directive 1979
- Water Resources Act 1991
- Pollution Prevention and Control Regulations 2000
- PPG 9: Nature Conservation
- PPG 13: Transport
- PPG 23: Planning and Pollution Control
- PPG 25: Development and Flood Risk

Key fact

There are important links between the planning system and other regulatory arrangements. Negotiations for the range of required consents should take place in parallel

Scoping

- location plan/site plan/outline development plan
- consultations undertaken (e.g. record correspondence, meetings, exhibitions)
- principal opinions (e.g. reports from statutory consultees, analysis of questionnaires)
- principal issues to be addressed
- outline of methodology for collating baseline information, assessing impact magnitude and significance, and identifying mitigation
- reasons for not addressing other issues.

The EIA guide to procedures (DETR 2000) provides a checklist of matters to be considered for inclusion when preparing an ES. These provide a useful guide to carrying out the scoping exercise.

Checklist of EIA Matters

Information describing the project:
- purpose and physical characteristics
- land-use requirements and physical features
- production processes and operational features: resource usage, residues and emissions
- alternative sites and processes, including 'do nothing' scenario.

Information describing the site and its environment:
- physical features
- policy framework.

Assessment of effects on:
- humans, buildings and man-made features
- flora, fauna and geology
- land
- water
- air and climate
- other indirect and secondary effects.

Mitigating measures: description and likely effectiveness.

Risks of accidents and hazardous development.

From DETR 2000

"

Assessment of effects should include:
- direct
- indirect
- secondary
- cumulative
- short, medium and long term
- permanent
- temporary
- positive
- negative

DETR 2000

"

The initial contact for scoping should be with the planning authority who can also advise on other interested parties to be consulted. It is helpful to provide the sort of information formally listed in the Regulations (see above) at this stage. Development team members should generally be able from experience and initial desk study and site survey to suggest most of the issues likely to arise in the locality concerned. Particular designations, e.g. AONB, SSSI, SAM will influence the type of issue to be addressed. This will enable some initial thoughts to be presented in the Scoping Report to the consultation bodies.

Key facts

- Not all the environmental matters will be relevant to any one project
- Effects before and during construction should be considered separately from operation/occupation and decommissioning
- Pre-construction effects can include: blight, off-site planting, ancillary developments, site preparation

The preparation of this can be facilitated through team discussion; checklists or matrices can be helpful to ensure nothing is missed.

Matrix of Issues for Scoping

environmental topic	effects						
	characteristic		scale*	significance			project phase
	adverse, beneficial, neutral	direct, indirect, cumulative	I, N, R, D, L	long-term, short-term	irreversible, reversible	major, minor	pre-construction construction operation/occupation decommissioning restoration
Population							
Transport							
Noise and vibration							
Biodiversity							
Soils, geology and agriculture							
Water							
Air, climate and odour							
Cultural heritage/ material assets							
Landscape							
Interactions							

*I: International, N: National, R: Regional, D: District, L: Local

Adapted from: DoE 1995, Preparing Environmental Statements for Planning Projects

If matrices or checklists are used, it is essential to keep them simple, since at this stage we are only looking for the potential key issues; details of significance can be addressed later. A pragmatic approach is to use professional expertise and consultation to scope the EIA and then use such matrices as a checklist to ensure that no important issues have been overlooked. A useful guide as to whether an issue should be included or not is to ask the question 'will anyone be concerned about this – who does it affect?'

While it is important to focus on these key issues, for some types of development, e.g. outline applications for mixed use development, it may be particularly difficult to eliminate any issues from consideration at this preliminary stage and it is necessary to keep all issues under examination. This is of particular relevance when a preferred alternative emerges part of the

guiding principle

Keep matrices and checklists simple

way through the assessment process. If scoping has been done thoroughly from the beginning no new issues should be raised.

If a scoping opinion is requested, then the proposals will enter the public domain via the consultation that a planning authority may undertake. Similarly, if the scheme proposals include a contentious licence required from the Environment Agency then it is Agency policy to involve the public at an early stage via public meetings or exhibitions. Therefore, scoping cannot be guaranteed to remain confidential and if commercial considerations are implicated, the preliminary scoping should be undertaken by the promoter's team alone.

The Scoping Exercise in Summary
- review relevant development plans
- review government and strategic policy guidance
- identify non-planning regulatory requirements
- determine initial list of potential issues
- request formal scoping opinion and/or consult with planning authority
- consult with statutory and non-statutory consultees
- prepare scoping report and agree with planning authority.

2.5 Consultation

Definition

Consultation is the process by which those organizations or individuals with an interest in the area proposed for development are identified, their opinions or concerns recorded and incorporated into the EIA. These consultees may also hold environmental information relating to the locality.

Legislation

Developers are under no formal obligation to consult prior to the submission of an application or authorization for development. There is a requirement for the authorizing authority to undertake formal consultation after submission of the ES.

Discussion

Consultation is inherent in the iterative EIA process. This approach ensures that the design project team is informed, practicable alternatives are properly considered, and delay due to redesign requirements is avoided.

The stages of consultation may conveniently be summarized as follows:

- Preliminary consultation: screening, scoping.
- EIA consultation: information, opinions, public consultation.
- Formal consultation: after ES submission.

---

guiding principle

Consult early; consult often

---

case example

Fulham Football Club

The club had applied for planning permission to build a new stadium, flats and a riverside walkway. An ES was not prepared. Consent was granted but then challenged on the grounds that the EIA Directive had not been followed. The House of Lords quashed the planning decision. Included in their reasoning was the fact that the Directive is rooted in rights of public consultation, which had not been followed.

(*Berkeley* v. *Secretary of State* 2000)

Preliminary Consultation

This relates to the screening and scoping phases as discussed in the preceding sections.

EIA Consultation

When it has been established that an EIA is required and that an ES will be prepared, the authorizing authority will notify the relevant statutory consultees (confirming this to the developer).

This formal notification obliges the consultees to provide the developer with such information as may be relevant to the preparation of the ES. (A reasonable charge for the information may be made.) It is then up to the developer to approach these consultees and indicate the type of information required.

Key facts
- Authorizing authority duties are to advise consultees that an EIA is being undertaken
- Consultees have a duty to provide information in their possession
- The developer is required to approach the consultees for the information

---

Statutory consultees for EIA (other relevant bodies and departments in Scotland, Wales and Northern Ireland)

- The relevant planning authority(ies)
- Countryside Agency
- English Nature
- Environment Agency
- Other bodies under General Development Procedure Order 1995.

Other bodies to be consulted depending on type of development or nature of land:

- Health and Safety Executive
- Department of Transport, Local Government and the Regions
- Coal Authority
- English Heritage (Historic Buildings and Monuments Commission for England)
- Department for Environment, Food and Rural Affairs
- Sports Council
- British Waterways.

(Wider consultation with non-statutory consultees may also be advisable since these sources may have particular knowledge and information.)

Sources of preliminary information to determine environmental sensitivity

- Local authority: local plan proposals, county wildlife sites, archaeological sites, historic maps, contaminated land.
- Environment Agency: Local Environment Agency Plans (LEAPs), Source Protection Zones (SPZs), Nitrate Sensitive Areas, Flood Risk Areas (S105 maps), Water Quality.

Consultation

> - English Nature: Sites of Special Scientific Interest (SSSIs), Natural Areas, Special Protection Areas (SPAs), Special Areas of Conservation (SACs).
> - Countryside Agency: Areas of Outstanding Natural Beauty (AONB), Landscape Character Areas.
> - English Heritage: Scheduled Ancient Monuments (SAMs).

Further information

1992 *Environmental Information Regulations*

guiding principle

Programme sufficient time for information retrieval

Information requests should include an indication of the proposals, a site location map, a specification of the information required, a date for reply and a request for an indication of any data retrieval costs. If information relates to protected species, then a commitment should be made to keep this separate from that publicly available in the ES.

It is essential to allow sufficient time in the project development programme for responses to such requests since, e.g. government departments and organizations may have different response times. Furthermore, the Environmental Information Regulations allow up to 2 months for the provision of information.

Non-statutory consultees include:

- Wildlife Trusts and other nature conservation groups.
- Royal Society for Protection of Birds (RSPB).
- Council for the Protection of Rural England (CPRE).
- Water Companies and other utilities.
- Community and Amenity Groups.
- Local history and geological societies.
- Society for Protection of Ancient Buildings (SPAB).
- National Society for Clean Air (NSCA).
- Recreation groups.

Generally, it is advantageous for developers to also seek opinions once the proposals are clear enough to form the basis for discussion. Such opinions can be requested in the information request letters or at meetings. All such communication may be requested to be 'in confidence' at this early stage if no formal scoping opinion has been sought.

Key fact

Concerns expressed during early consultation can be incorporated in evolving design

guiding principle

Use exhibitions and questionnaires for most effective public consultation

While under no obligation to publicize the proposals there can be advantages to gauge general opinion and local concerns at this early stage: mitigation can be designed in if concerns are recognized early enough. It is important to manage this process carefully and, if opinions are to be sought, begin with local authority planners and members before going public. There are various techniques available for public consultation but the most productive medium for public information and participation is via exhibitions and questionnaires. Public meetings allow the most vocal to create uneven representation, bias and conflict (for communication and initial consultation see also Section 2.2).

Formal Consultation

Once the ES is submitted with the application for development, then the formal consultation can begin. The preceding informal discussions will help facilitate timely responses. The Regulations make the following provisions:

Outline of formal provisions for consultation according to EIA Regulations

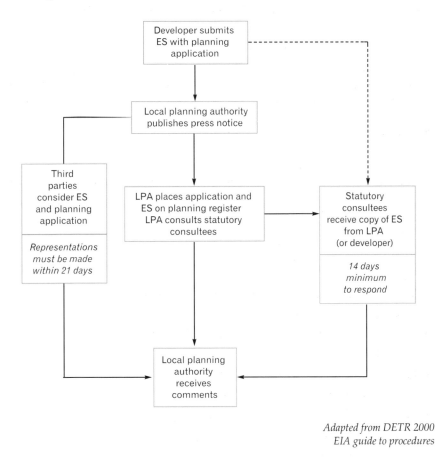

Adapted from DETR 2000
EIA guide to procedures

Consultation in Summary

- Consultation lies at the root of the EIA process: to gather information and to identify concerns.
- Early consultation allows concerns to be addressed and the scheme design adapted to incorporate mitigation.
- Time should be allowed in the EIA process for adequate consultation and responses.

2.6   Baseline Studies

Definition

Baseline studies describe the current (and predicted – see Discussion below) condition of those elements of the environment which are likely to be significantly affected by the proposed development. The baseline

Baseline Studies

environmental conditions should be evaluated according to their importance and sensitivity. This can be achieved by reference to relevant designations and standards. Baseline conditions can be described and evaluated using existing data but may require further surveys and studies to be undertaken.

Legislation

The Regulations do not specifically refer to 'baseline studies', however, the need for such data to identify and assess the main environmental effects is a minimum requirement (Schedule 4, Part II). The Regulations require an indication of any difficulties (technical deficiencies or lack of know-how) encountered during compilation of the required information.

Discussion

An environmental impact is a change in an aspect of the environment which is predicted to occur over a particular time period and within a defined area as a result of the construction and operation of the proposed development. The question of what is the relevant baseline arises. It is recognized that neither the natural nor the human environments are static. For example, a wood develops through growth and succession, a town grows as a result of population growth. The baseline studies should, therefore, be based on the predicted condition of the environment at the time of the proposed development, e.g. if a new harbour is to be built, the geomorphological studies for an EIA for coastal defences should be based on the 'with harbour' situation.

The level of information also has to be appropriate for the development proposed. There have probably been more legal challenges on this question than any other. Recent case law indicates that there is a need now to provide far more information than was the original minimalist approach envisaged by the UK government in the 1980s.

It is, therefore, necessary for the developer, consultants and the regulators to carefully consider and agree the level of detail appropriate to a particular development (this applies to the description of the project as well as the environmental information; see Section 4.2). The test is that it should be sufficient to assess the significant impacts – planning consent cannot be granted without it – regardless of whether it is for an outline or detailed application.

The issues, their relative importance and their boundaries for which such information is to be provided, should be detailed at the scoping stage and through consultation. They should be drawn widely enough to cover indirect effects, cumulative effects and alternative sites that may be suggested during the consultation process.

Key fact

The information required should have regard to current knowledge and methods, and be such that the applicant could **reasonably** be required to compile

case example

The EIA for an inner city regeneration project had to take into account the additional traffic and emissions generated by an adjacent, but not yet built, supermarket with planning permission granted.

guiding principle

Judicial Review decisions have emphasized the need to provide sufficient information in order to assess the environmental effects

case example

The ES for an extension to a landfill site recorded that while no bats had been found during survey the habitat was suitable for bats and further surveys were recommended. English Nature and Cornwall Wildlife Trust were content that permission should be granted subject to a condition requiring such survey. Since the bats were specifically protected by European Directives, the ES was held to be defective since it did not contain sufficient information about the baseline environmental conditions or the significant adverse effects of the project.

R. v. Cornwall County Council

Methodology

Baseline studies may generally be initiated through desk studies of existing information generated as a result of the scoping exercise. This confirms the key issues and the level of detail required for particular issues. The need for further field surveys is then identified. At an early stage, consideration should be given to any seasonal constraints or requirements for survey – specialist fauna and flora surveys may only be relevant at certain times of the year, and visual impact assessment may require photomontages during both summer and winter – sufficient time should be programmed into the project for such surveys.

It does have to be emphasized that baseline studies are not intended to fall into the category of 'original research'. Experts can predict how particular habitats will react or develop and surveys can be selected to provide accurate information, e.g. a chemical survey will do little more than provide a snapshot of the water quality of a river, whereas a biological (which may be more expensive and constrained by seasons) survey can provide a more accurate assessment of long-term conditions.

The field studies and their interpretation can be developed and refined as the iterative process of EIA unfolds. (Developers and regulators should also be aware of the need for assessment under other European Directives and the necessary scope of the baseline studies.)

When designing the baseline studies methods, it is necessary to consider the relevant environmental boundaries and the interactions of the environmental topics. For example, impacts on water resources may be best considered at the regional level, while surface water drainage and flood risk effects are likely to be local or at river catchment level. The interactions with traffic, noise and air quality are so inter-related that the traffic studies need to be designed to provide the necessary baseline for air quality and noise predictions as well as traffic numbers. Similarly, baseline drainage studies designed to assess flood risk effects may need to consider water quality and ecological parameters.

Baseline studies should be designed and undertaken in such a way that they can be replicated during any post-construction monitoring exercise.

guiding principle
Programme sufficient time for seasonal surveys

case example
Minehead Coastal Defences
The local authority archaeologist required full information on the nature and condition of mediaeval fish weirs before approval could be granted for new coastal defences. These could only be examined during daylight and at extreme low tide and the project was delayed by several months as a result.

Baseline Studies in Summary

- All parties should agree the scope and depth required of baseline studies in order to properly assess the effects of development.
- The baseline should consider future developments, natural processes, other consented developments, as well as the 'do nothing' scenario.
- Project management should programme time for seasonal surveys.
- Baseline studies are not research studies.
- Baseline studies should be broad enough to consider emerging alternative development sites/processes.
- Study methods progress from scoping to desk and field studies and are designed to be readily replicable.

2.7   Impact Assessment and Significance

Definition

Impact assessment refers to the change that is predicted to take place to the existing condition of the environment as a result of the proposed development. Significance is judged by comparing the extent of the change with particular standards and criteria relevant to each environmental topic. For example, concentrations of a chemical emission will double (the change or impact); this will result in exceeding an air quality objective leading to potential harm to health (the significance of the effect).

Legislation

The Regulations require a description of the likely significant effects of the proposed project on the environment resulting from the:

- existence of the project
- use of natural resources
- emission of pollutants, the creation of nuisances and the elimination of waste.

The potential significant effects of projects must be considered in relation to the characteristics and location of the project, with particular regard to the:

- extent of the impact (geographical area and size of affected population)
- transfrontier nature of the impact
- magnitude and complexity of the impact
- duration, frequency and reversibility of the impact.

Furthermore, the predictive methods used to assess the effects on the environment should be described.

The description of the effects should address:

- direct, indirect and secondary
- cumulative
- short, medium and long term
- permanent and temporary
- positive and negative.

Discussion

'Significance' in EIA is a judgement based on the:

- context in which the impact is likely to occur
- intensity or severity of the impact
- importance to the community and consultees of the resulting effect.

This last point highlights the fact that significance is, as some authors maintain, essentially anthropocentric. While science can often describe an impact with some reasonable accuracy, and EIA has developed as a process to present and communicate the findings of studies, development proposals have to take political acceptability and promotability into account.

Impacts and their significance should be clearly stated avoiding the use of palliative phrases of which the readers will be justifiably suspicious. Similarly, transparency of sources, judgements and any uncertainties will generate confidence in the conclusions reached. Predictions should be based on a reasonable worst-case scenario to comply with the precautionary principle of sustainable development.

Significance is often subjective and professionals may well disagree but the community may be more prepared to accept and approve projects which will relieve unemployment or where inward investment is needed despite negative environmental impacts. This does not detract from the judgement of the significance of the effect with regard to the environment. It can be particularly relevant where component or cumulative effects are indicated.

The increasing requirement for improved community and neighbourhood participation in the UK land-use planning process has also driven the development of new techniques and approaches in assessing what is important to the public. For example, 'Environmental Capital – What Matters and Why' (Countryside Agency *et al.* 1999) was developed for the environmental regulators and then evolved into the 'Quality of Life Capital' (2001) to encompass the three elements of sustainable development. The EA is developing an environmental capacity approach which considers the capacity of the receiving environment to absorb land-use change.

Key fact

Significance is influenced by the values of individuals and how the project or the changes in the environment are perceived to affect them

case example

Minehead Sea Defences

Community consultation and participation in the EIA process for a flood defence scheme for a coastal community identified that the preservation of fish weirs (which still provided a livelihood to some families in the community and were also of archaeological interest) were a key consideration in the acceptability of the scheme options.

Photo by Graham Sizer

Impact Assessment and Significance

"
The intrusion of wider public concerns and social values is inescapable and contentions will remain even with well defined criteria and a structured approach.

– Sadler 1996

"

---

case example

Gas-powered Power Station

A gas-powered station was proposed to replace a redundant coal-fired plant. Separate ESs were produced for the proposed 40 km gas pipeline, the power station itself, and the electricity transmission lines to the national grid. While the local authority where the power station was proposed was very keen to grant approval, the Dti (the authorizing body) had to take account of the overall development which affected neighbouring communities and planning authorities,

---

guiding principle

A systematic approach, clarity and transparency are vital

Avoid confusing the characteristics and magnitude of the impact with its significance

Acknowledge uncertainty and margins of error associated with impact prediction

---

case example

Inner City Regeneration

An EIA for a mixed use inner city regeneration project identified at the first stage listed buildings and parks in the locality but it took discussion with the local history society to realize that a fountain in the park had been erected by the founder of a disused factory. This had been an important local employer and the community would have been most upset if plans had involved its removal

---

Methodology

There are two stages in assessment of the significance of impacts. The first stage characterizes the nature of the impact (e.g. $10\,dB_A$ increase over $100\,m$ for x receptors) and then the second stage determines the significance (e.g. this exceeds a set EQS or it will affect a particularly sensitive receptor such as a hospital).

The determination of significance ultimately relies on professional judgement, although exceedence of standards, criteria and thresholds can help guide this judgement. Such standards are different for each environmental topic and details of these and methodologies are given in Chapter 3.

However, a simple matrix is often used to give an early indication of the degree of significance of any impact.

Scale \ Magnitude	Low	Medium	High
Local			
County			
Regional			
National			
International			

Impacts should be considered for each phase of a project:

- construction
- operation/occupation
- restoration
- decommissioning.

This model is also particularly useful as a quick way of comparing the merits of alternatives. For example, the effects of development on statutorily designated areas such as SAMs will provide a broad indication of significance. However, the effects on features which are not on any register can be important to local neighbourhoods and their identification at an early stage is essential. The success of this stage of the EIA, therefore, relies on thorough consultation.

Impact Assessment and Significance in Summary

Good practice for impact assessment and significance requires:

- a systematic approach, carefully organized, managed and recorded
- understandable method, clearly stated, reproducible and verifiable
- description of the basis on which judgements are made
- where difficulties are encountered or the impact predictions rely on subjectivity or are unquantifiable, this should be stated
- assumptions made and levels of confidence to be stated.

2.8   Mitigation

Definition

Mitigation has been defined in UK government research as 'measures which are incorporated into the design or implementation of a development project for the purpose of avoiding, reducing, remedying or compensating for its adverse environmental impacts. It may also include measures to create environmental benefits' (DETR 1997). The distinction between compensation, remediation and enhancement is often not clearly defined or understood.

Legislation

The EC Directive and the Regulations require 'a description of the measures envisaged in order to avoid, to reduce and if possible remedy significant adverse effects'.

Discussion

The purpose of addressing mitigation is to develop a scheme which aims to progress towards 'no net loss' effect on the environment.

The Regulations allow for a hierarchy of mitigation, however sustainability principles require avoidance or compensation to achieve no net loss to the environment.

Mitigation as part of the EIA process plays a key role in terms of sustainability since it addresses issues such as resource usage, capacity and biodiversity within a project life cycle framework.

Mitigation is for negative impacts: other environmental measures might be enhancement, planning gain or compensation in kind; mitigation is, by definition, focused on identified negative impacts.

Methodology

The descriptions of the mitigation proposed need to be precise and clearly stated if a planning authority is to rely upon them for setting planning conditions in any subsequent approval. If the descriptions are clearly related to the potential impacts of the scheme before mitigation, then the likely benefits can be predicted; the degree of confidence in the effectiveness of the mitigation proposed should be stated – the monitoring to check and correct the effects should also be stated. Finally, the impacts remaining after mitigation and for which no mitigation is proposed or possible – the residual impacts – should be clearly identified. Any uncertainty should be reported and measures to correct unforeseen consequences stated.

It must be remembered that the mitigation process is an iterative one which is continuous throughout the project design development. Each stage should be reported to and recorded by the EIA co-ordinator for inclusion in the ES. The identification and incorporation of mitigation can only be effective if the EIA co-ordinator is engaged from the start.

References
DETR 1997, Mitigation Measures in Environmental Statements

Key fact
Mitigation hierarchy:
- Avoid
- Reduce
- Remedy

Key fact
Mitigation is the principal design tool in Environmental Impact Assessment

guiding principle

The ES should specify for each mitigation option:
- who is responsible
- what will be done
- when it will be done
- how it will be achieved
- how effective it will be

Key fact
Requirements under other legislation such as environmental protection are not considered to be mitigation, e.g. a bund to contain chemical or oil spillages is not mitigation

guiding principle

EIA is an iterative process and mitigation should be designed in, not 'bolted on'

Mitigation

To identify whether mitigation is actually necessary cross reference to the environmental risk assessment exercise should be carried out. Risk assessment is a management tool that aids decision making; it considers the likelihood, the consequences of an event and how best to manage any unacceptable risks. This will have identified impacts, their probability and their severity so that it can then be decided at what level of probability/impact mitigation should be triggered. If this is implemented throughout the design process the impacts will be minimized – remembering to mitigate for cumulative and indirect impacts.

Risk Assessment is a management tool that aids decision making and is increasingly used by the environmental regulators. It involves the consideration of the likelihood and the consequences of an event, and how best to manage any unacceptable risks. Environmental risk assessment requires an understanding of the:

- source of a hazard (e.g. a chemical that can cause harm) to, or from, the environment
- characteristics of an environmental receptor (e.g. human, ecosystem)
- means, or pathway (e.g. the air, groundwater) by which the receptor may be affected by that hazard.

Adapted from Environment Agency 2000

Key fact

Environmental regulation is based on risk assessment and management

Further information

COMAH and COSHH Regulations

Health and Safety at Work Regulations

DETR, Environment Agency, CIEH, 2000, *Guidelines for Environmental Risk Assessment and Management*

Royal Commission on Environmental Pollution 21st Report, Setting Environmental Standards, 1998

EA, SEPA, DoE NI, 2002 Risk Assessment for Environmental Professionals

Mitigation Strategy

Projects which comply with policy and have minimal impact on the environment are most likely to achieve planning consent. Mitigation should be considered at the commencement of the project design and in this respect choice of site and/or process can play an important part by avoiding or minimizing the impact and thus reducing the need for mitigation. These considerations should be set out in the ES in a transparent and methodical way. There is a requirement to describe alternatives in the ES (see Section 2.9).

Options for mitigation:

- strategic
- design
- management.

Strategic mitigation will consider the alternative sites or processes available. The first step is to consider alternative ways of achieving the stated objective of the project. Using leakage control or public education to reduce water demand thus obviating the need for a new high impact reservoir is an example of strategic mitigation cited by government (DETR 1997).

The second step is to consider alternative sites which avoid or reduce the significance of a potential impact. Continuing with the example of the reservoir, a location outside of environmentally designated areas may be considered. This should be stated in the ES even if the location is rejected on other grounds, e.g. safety, economic.

Finally a different process may be considered – again the provision of water may be sourced by desalination plant or river regulation and abstraction.

Mitigation through design is implemented once the strategic decisions on the method, site and process have been determined.

In the case of a reservoir, the dam may be curved to reflect its surroundings, shallows may be provided for wildfowl, construction access roads may be built below final top water level, or new woodland may be planted to replace that lost as a result of the development.

Mitigation by management is the final level of mitigation. This will include such measures as dust control during construction or operation, working hours, reporting and control of pollution incidents. These are most usefully scheduled in the environmental management section of the ES and can, therefore, act as a checklist for conditions to be imposed by planning authorities as well as a schedule for contractors to take into consideration when tendering for the construction contract. A contractor having a formal EMS can assist the confidence levels of regulators in this respect – in the knowledge that auditing, monitoring and remedial action will take place.

guiding principle

Make clear commitment to mitigation

Mitigation Hierarchy

The approach is to avoid impacts and if they cannot be avoided, to reduce them. If impacts still remain then the next option is to remedy the damage or to compensate for it. It is often held that compensation is only true mitigation if it genuinely replaces what is lost. New planting in place of ancient woodland which will be destroyed as a result of the development will obviously not be a totally satisfactory substitute.

All options for mitigation should be considered at all stages of the potential project – construction, operation/occupation, decommissioning, restoration.

Mitigation Hierarchy	
Option	*Example*
Avoid at source	Avoid machinery
Minimize impacts at source	Use quiet machinery
Abate impacts on site	Use acoustic barriers
Abate impacts at receptor	Provide double glazing
Repair impacts	Monitor and remedy
Compensate in kind	Move residents for duration of construction
Other compensation and enhancement	Liaise with residents

guiding principle

Aim for mitigation option towards the top of the hierarchy

Adapted from DETR 1997

Choosing an option as high up the hierarchy as possible is in accordance with the EU Directive which states that community policy on the environment is based on the following principles:

- precautionary principle
- preventative action should be taken

■ environmental damage should be rectified at source
■ the polluter should pay.

Commitment to Mitigation

The authorizing bodies and regulators must remember that mitigation measures are only enforceable if they are included in the planning permission or other authorization via conditions: their inclusion in the ES alone is not enough to guarantee their implementation. Another option is to use planning agreements (or obligations) under which the developer and the planning authority enter into a contract to restrict use of land, undertake specific operations on the land or make payments to the authority to provide facilities which are needed to enable the development to proceed.

Mitigation that is suggested in the event that its requirement becomes apparent subsequently is termed deferred mitigation. For example, a watching brief for archaeological remains will be provided and archaeological investigations undertaken if anything is found during the watching brief.

The developer can also demonstrate a commitment to mitigation through an Environmental Management Plan (EMP) – introduced in the ES. A schedule of environmental commitments offers a useful method of clarifying the mitigation measures that a developer is committed to and can be progressively updated as the project design evolves. Means of implementation and enforcement should be described.

Mitigation in Summary

■ Consult early to identify mitigation opportunities.
■ Consider mitigation from earliest stage of project identification.
■ Select mitigation as high up the hierarchy as possible.
■ Review mitigation options at all stages of the design, construction and management process.
■ Clearly state mitigation considered, its likely effectiveness and monitoring proposed.
■ Commit to mitigation that will be implemented and monitored – via EMP.
■ State measures to correct unforeseen consequences.

2.9   Alternatives

Definition

There is a legal requirement to address alternatives but there is no statutory EIA definition of 'alternatives' and so it is open to interpretation. It is usually taken to be the examination of alternative approaches to deliver the scheme objectives and alternative sites, processes or management:

Alternative ways of achieving the objective, e.g. leakage control rather than new reservoir.

Alternative means, e.g. different locations for reservoir or several reservoirs.

Legislation

Schedule 4 of the Regulations requires an outline of the main alternatives studied by the applicant or appellant and an indication of the main reasons for this choice, taking into account the environmental effects.

Discussion

The reasons for examination, recording and reporting of alternatives considered at all stages of the EIA process are closely linked and such methodologies have been described in Section 2.8: alternative approaches may result in a viable, practicable scheme that is more acceptable in environmental terms. Methods of evaluating significance also indicate useful ways of comparing alternatives (Section 2.7).

DETR Circular 02/99 states that the Directive and the Regulations 'do not expressly require the developer to study alternatives'. This may appear to be at variance with Schedule 4 of the Regulations and the explanation is that alternatives must be outlined and reasons for the final choice given *where alternative approaches to development have been considered.* So developers are encouraged to consider alternatives, if they do so they must report them but if they are not considered it does not nullify the ES. Notwithstanding this, good practice recognizes that consideration of alternatives facilitates the decision-making process. It is recognized that options may be limited, e.g. mineral extraction schemes – but the Circular advises that the nature and location of some developments may make consideration of alternative sites a material consideration – however, case law indicates that this is only in exceptional circumstances.

Government has always emphasized the benefits of starting the EIA process at the inception of projects which allows for full consideration of alternatives – site, process or procedures – because it adds to the credibility and objectives of the ES. This can demonstrate that environmental factors have been taken into account throughout the project design process.

When deciding at what level of detail to study with respect to alternatives, the best guidance is to investigate only those which are 'practical', i.e. those fulfilling the criteria of 'need' and 'purpose', i.e. keep the development objectives clear.

The advice is to start the examination of alternatives early, but how early? If house builders are proposing a housing development, in accordance with a local authority allocation, they cannot be expected to examine alternative locations – these should be evaluated at an earlier stage using SEA at the development plan preparation stage. Policy evaluation is outside the scope of private developers.

However, what house builders **can** study is, e.g. alternatives in housing density, mix, infrastructure provision and masterplan and detail design.

> **Consideration of alternatives ... results in a more robust application for planning permission**
> – DETR 2000

Alternatives

Approach and Methodology

Stages in the analysis of broad alternatives are shown below:

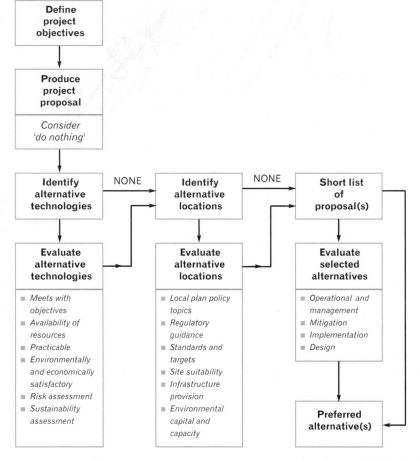

Adapted from World Bank 1996

Alternatives: Technologies

The sewerage system of a major city was over 100 years old and combined sewer overflows were subject to premature and frequent operation causing pollution and affecting amenity and recreation. Updating of the system was required to meet the standards of the urban wastewater treatment directive. The responsible water undertaker commissioned feasibility studies which examined a range of alternative options for treatment, storage and transmission of sewage, including EIA of these options.

Alternatives: Locations

A coastal conurbation had limited sewage treatment facilities, discharging screened sewage to the marine environment. An assessment was undertaken of alternative locations for a new sewage treatment works. Criteria for the suitability of such sites were set which were based on availability, local plan policy issues, and regulatory constraints. The site which the water undertaking and the planning authority agreed had the least environmental impact was strongly opposed by the local residents and the 'second best' site had to be promoted and eventually approved.

Having selected this short list of practicable alternative proposals, they are then examined in terms of their respective design, construction and operational alternatives taking mitigation into account. At this stage it is useful to hold an exhibition explaining the various identified options and inviting public comment – recorded by means of questionnaires – but note that the views of the majority may not necessarily reflect the best practicable environmental option. It is then for the planning authorities and regulators to explain their views. This systematic approach will identify the most robust development option – the process should be fully documented and reported in the ES. It is essential to be clear about the use of the criteria – which can be those presenting opportunities, e.g. near to major transport route as well as constraints, e.g. near to educational establishment.

Alternatives in Summary

- Description of alternatives studied is mandatory.
- Alternatives can refer to locations, processes or procedures.
- The criteria for assessing alternatives should be clear.

2.10 Monitoring

Definitions

- **Monitoring** comprises the collection of data or information on a range of specific environmental variables. It is subject to a time-related programme of measurements or observations.
- **Auditing** is the comparison of monitoring results with criteria or predictions. It may also relate to, and be a requirement of, an organization's environmental management system (EMS) (e.g. ISO 14001 EMS) or policy.

Legislation

There is no specific requirement in the Directive or the Regulations to undertake monitoring. However, if the planning authority, other regulators or consultees consider it necessary and appropriate then this could be made a specific request at the scoping stage.

In order to secure a commitment to monitoring, the planning authority may use planning conditions or obligations. Other regulators may require monitoring under other legislation and planning authorities should not duplicate such requirements.

The Circular 02/99 refers to the fact that developers can apply or adopt EMSs to demonstrate implementation of mitigation measures and to monitor their effectiveness.

Discussion

Monitoring can be undertaken at various stages of the EIA process. In the first instance, **baseline monitoring** may be required in order to assess or predict potential effects and to provide the basis for comparison with later, **post-construction monitoring**. This is essentially undertaken for two principal reasons:

- **Compliance monitoring** to ensure commitments to mitigation or predictions are met.
- **Effects monitoring** to correct unforeseen negative effects of development.

Compliance monitoring may also be undertaken in order to comply with other regulatory consents or licences: in this instance it may be undertaken by other regulators.

It is clear that monitoring can be put in place to ensure that mitigation is achieved – and that, as stated above, this can be achieved via conditions or agreements. It is essential that the planning authorities or other regulators ensure that they have the resources to undertake and enforce such monitoring; a commitment to provision of such resources could be included in the conditions.

The results of monitoring on a project by a developer can be fed into the design of future projects and also improve the quality of future ESs.

case example

Wytch Farm Oilfield

This development, the largest on-shore oilfield in Western Europe at the time of its proposal by BP Exploration, was set in an area of considerable environmental sensitivity and tourism activity. The local planning authority were concerned that above ground elements should either not be visible from publicly accessible viewpoints or should not be intrusive in the view. Planning approval was granted and appropriate conditions were imposed. During construction and operation of the oilfield the planning officers regularly monitored the visibility of activities to confirm:

- the predictions of the EIA
- compliance with conditions.

Corrective actions were applied if necessary.

*Monitoring/Environmental
Statement*

Again, although not a requirement, feedback from residents or affected communities will be useful to ensure that issues are identified and corrective action taken and also to be able to demonstrate to other communities best practice and actual effects.

Methodology

The monitoring proposals should be explained in the ES and drawn together in the Environmental Management section of the ES (see Chapter 5). The monitoring plan describes what is undertaken, who undertakes it, how and when.

It should, therefore, specify:

- the indicators selected for monitoring
- the measurement technique
- frequency
- location
- responsibilities
- the range of data to be collected.

The purpose of the monitoring should be decided in advance. For any identified environmental issue the methodology should be clearly focused on the effects which will be attributable to the development rather than other external or natural pressures or changes.

The auditing report should include:

- the results of monitoring
- how this compares to baseline
- how this compares to standards and conditions
- corrective action
- recommendations for further monitoring.

Monitoring in Summary

- Monitoring is used to ensure compliance with planning consents or conditions, regulatory requirements or to check the effectiveness of mitigation.
- It provides a means of correcting any unforeseen impacts.
- Monitoring should be clearly focused on its objectives.
- Monitoring should be committed to in the Environmental Management section of the ES and may be linked to the developer's EMS.

2.11 Environmental Statement: Preparation, Content and Review

Introduction

The preceding sections in this chapter have outlined the various components of the EIA process. This section summarizes the procedural process

guiding principle

Monitoring proposals need to be explicit and targeted

To be effective, the predictions in the ES need to be quantified highlighting the various legislative requirements and possibilities. It suggests a format for the ES itself and finally introduces various review methods for checking the quality of the ES. These review methods may be used by developers, their consultants, local authorities or local communities to ensure that the ES is a robust statement of environmental effects of the proposal.

Legislation

The various procedures required during the EIA process are discussed in DETR Circular 02/99 EIA and in *Environmental Impact Assessment: A guide to procedures* (DETR 2000).

The required contents of an ES are presented in the Regulations Schedule 4 which is reproduced here in Appendix 3 for ease of reference. Schedule 4 is in two parts: Part I describes such information as may reasonably be required and Part II indicates the minimum information which must be reported in an ES.

Summary of formal preparation procedures

- **Screening:**
  - Deciding if EIA is legally required.*
  - Is it a Schedule 1 or 2 development?
  - If Schedule 2, is it in a sensitive area or likely to exceed the threshold of significance?

- **Planning authority** informs statutory consultees of the intended proposal.

- **Scoping:**
  - Identifying the topics to be addressed in the EIA and reported in the ES.

- **Consultation:**
  - Initial consideration of alternatives and mitigation.
  - Provision of available environmental information to developer by statutory consultees.
  - Consultation with statutory, non-statutory consultees and general public.
  - Consideration of exhibitions and other publicity.

- **Environmental Statement with Non-technical Summary** to planning or regulatory authority.

*Note that any permitted development rights, e.g. in the case of a statutory undertaker, do not apply if EIA is required. Screening can also be directed by the Secretary of State.

Format and Content of Environmental Statement

There are no statutory requirements for the format of an ES but it must contain the minimum information in Schedule 4 of the Regulations (see Appendix 3).

Environmental Statement

A suggested format for an ES which includes all the items as may reasonably be required and which is compatible with the review criteria (see below) as used by the Institute of Environmental Management and Assessment is as follows:

1. Non-technical Summary	Included within ES and available separately the preparation of a NTS is a statutory requirement. Written in plain English. This should reflect the structure contents and findings of the ES itself. It should not be a promotional leaflet – but can legitimately include information about the applicant. It should include contact details for the applicant. It should be illustrated with at least a location map and site plan of the development.
2. Introduction	This should give details of the EIA team. Consultation undertaken including any public exhibitions. Structure of the ES. Contact details of the applicant.
3. Description of the Project	Size, scale, physical characteristics, proposed land uses and infrastructure. Discussion of need and alternatives considered. Programme, phasing, materials, resources, emissions.
4. Scoping	How the key issues discussed in the ES were identified. Copy of Scoping Report (or included as an appendix).
5. Planning Context	A description of the plans and policies which are relevant to the development. This should include development plans (local and regional), government guidance, national or international policies, advice given by statutory environmental agencies.
6. Assessment of Environmental Effects	This should include an analysis for each topic (as identified in the scoping process): – methodology – baseline conditions – potential effects and significance – mitigation – residual effects – enhancement proposals – monitoring.
7. Environmental Management	This draws together the environmental commitments made in the ES and provides an overall description of how the project would be managed throughout construction, operation/occupation and decommissioning/restoration where appropriate. It includes an outline EMP which can be used by planning authorities for identification of potential planning conditions and by contractors as an indication of environmental requirements. It addresses the overall cumulative impacts and acts in effect as a mitigation strategy.
8. Residual Impacts and Interactions Summary	
9. Appendices	Bibliography or references used. Abbreviations used in the ES. Glossary – this should be relatively brief since the document should be understandable to the non-specialist. Technical appendices – details of technical data.
10. Figures	Plans, maps, illustrations to accompany Sections 1–8.

The assessment of individual topics is described in Chapter 3 but the description of the project itself is important and discussed in Chapter 4. The following is a checklist of items to be included focusing throughout on those elements of the development which could have an environmental effect.

1. **Nature, purpose, need**
   - Function and economic context.
   - Alternatives considered – strategic, process, locations and criteria for choice.

2. **Land-use context**
   - Broad description of the site and its environs.
   - Topography and location.
   - Other similar developments in the locality.

3. **Characteristics of the development**
   - Size, layout, building and landscape design.
   - Traffic and transport links.
   - Utilities.
   - Employment – during construction and operation/occupation.
   - Operational hours and procedures.

4. **Programme and phasing (including alternative options)**
   - Construction:
     - frequency of operations that may cause nuisance
     - traffic
     - materials.
   - Operation/occupation:
     - number of occupiers, employees
     - traffic
     - resource, energy used
     - materials.
   - Decommissioning.
   - Restoration.

This section should be richly illustrated with photographs, maps, figures, plans, sketch impressions or photomontages of the proposals.

The ES itself can follow any format; common formats are:

- single A4 document with appendices and including illustrations
- A4 document with accompanying A3 landscape appendix for illustrations.

Recent ESs have been produced as CDs.

Whatever format is selected each volume should be clearly annotated to indicate the overall ES structure, e.g. Non-technical Summary Vol. 1 of 3 (Vol. 2, ES; Vol. 3, Appendices). Ideally the ES itself should be a 'stand

Environmental Statement

case example

Rochdale

Rochdale MBC gave outline planning consent for development of a business park on a greenfield site outside Rochdale on the basis of being in accordance with local plan policy. The decision was challenged in the High Court by third parties on the grounds of insufficient information. It was held that EIA is carried out on development **proposed** not on development which **might** be carried out. The result of this is that screening and scoping opinions and EIA for outline applications for urban development must be provided **with sufficient details of the project** to predict whether there will be significant effects.

The revised application with an extended ES was submitted. It was challenged again on the basis of non accordance with the development plan since certain elements relating to plan policy were still absent. It was held that proposals in accordance with the plan **as a whole** are sufficient and do not have to accord with every policy.

R. v. Rochdale MBC 1999, 2000

alone' document without the need to refer to other documentation. It should be visually attractive and easy to read and understand.

There are no limits to the length of ESs but good practice experience indicates that they should be between 150 and 200 pages in length. This length ensures that the ES is readable without becoming cumbersome; technical detail can be reported in appendices. They can be longer for complex projects involving multiple issues. ESs of less than 50 pages are unlikely to have examined the issues in sufficient detail.

Level of detail: In all cases, whether for a detailed or an outline application, sufficient information must be provided in the ES for the determining authorities and regulators to reach a reasoned decision on the acceptability of the proposals.

Timescale: This should include the:

– construction period
– time through to full occupation or operation
– time for mitigation to be effective, e.g. planting to mature
– restoration or decommissioning if appropriate.

Style: While the NTS has to be readable by the general public the ES itself has to be understandable by the non-specialist. This can best be achieved by avoiding the use of jargon and by clearly explaining technical terms in a glossary.

The ES should be unbiased and objective, with any qualitative statements defined, e.g. a 'minimal' visual impact could be defined as affecting no public views. Remember an ES 'accompanies' a planning application, it is not a 'supporting document'. At all times the audience should be borne in mind.

Reviewing the Quality of Environmental Statements

If the accompanying ES is considered inadequate, it will not necessarily invalidate the planning application; further information can be requested. If substantial further information is requested by the planning authority but not then provided by the applicant, the application can be refused on these grounds. The majority of local authorities have limited experience as to what to expect from an ES. For this reason a number of review packages (which have been developed out of research into ES quality) are available. The most commonly cited is Lee and Colley (1990, 1992), Reviewing the Quality of ESs. The Institute of Environmental Management and Assessment is frequently and regularly engaged to independently review the quality of ESs and they use their own package initially based on Lee and Colley. Both packages have been updated and revised.

The review criteria used in such packages are reproduced as Appendix 4.

ESs are reviewed independently by two reviewers who then compare and collate results.

As well as being of assistance to planning and regulatory authorities, the review process often helps the applicant as an internal audit on the content and adequacy of the ES.

Further information

www.iema.net
EIA Review Check List 2001 europa.eu.int

A major criticism of review packages is that, having been set up to review quality they tend not to encourage innovation in EIA technique since ESs became standardized in order to conform with the package. However, since such packages were introduced the overall quality has improved – although whether this is due to the review process or the greater experience of applicants and their advisors is a matter of conjecture.

Committee Report

Having received the planning application, the ES and any review, the local authority planning case officer will make a report and recommendation to committee. The structure of such a report is facilitated and can be guided by a competently prepared ES. Typically it might be as follows:

- summary
- background
- the site and its environs
- development proposals
- planning context – compliance with policy
- summary of environmental impacts
- views of consultees and public
- views of other authorities
- planning officer's comments
- recommendation.

ES Preparation, Content and Review in Summary

- Plain English and readable.
- Appropriate length with technical details in separate appendices.
- In sufficient detail to assess significant impacts – whether detailed or outline application.
- Consider internal or external audit review.

2.12   Environmental Statement: Submission

The EIA Regulations allow for an ES to be submitted with or after the planning application. It is in the developer's interest to submit an ES at the same time as the planning application since this will facilitate decision making as soon as possible. The LPA may decide to suspend consideration of the application until the ES is submitted. *If an ES is submitted after the application, the applicant rather than the LPA becomes responsible for publicity.* This section is concerned with planning regulations; the determining process varies with other regulations and determining bodies and authorities.

When an ES is submitted at the same time as the planning application, the developer must also submit a number of other copies of the ES:

- sufficient to send one to each of the statutory consultees
- three copies for the LPA to send to the Secretary of State

guiding principle

Programme timescale for decision making into project schedule.

*Environmental Statement:
Submission*

■ copies for the general public (a reasonable charge may be made and £50 was typical in 2001)

■ copies of the non-technical summary freely available.

Submission of ES with Planning Application

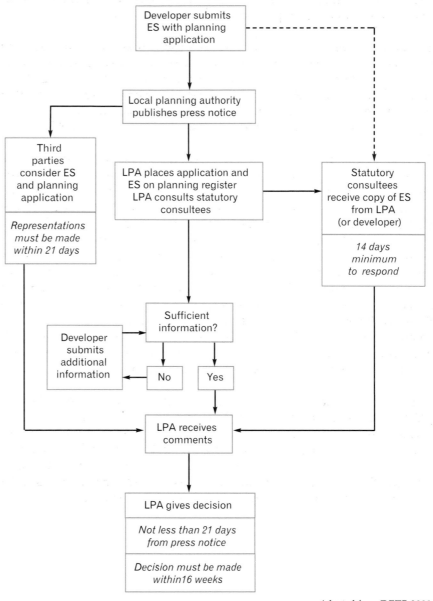

*Adapted from DETR 2000
EIA A guide to procedures*

The LPA must publicize receipt of the ES and application as follows:

■ notice in local newspaper

■ notice at or near the site of the proposed development.

■ place application and ES on the planning register

■ notify and send the ES to the statutory consultees

■ place the ES in an accessible location, e.g. at the LPA's offices, public library, post office, for consideration by the general public.

Key fact

Notices should include:

■ details of the ES
■ where available
■ timescale for receiving comments
■ charge for ES
■ address for comments

Environmental Statement:
Submission

The developer may send copies of the ES directly to the consultees. When submitting the application, the developer must inform the LPA of all names (statutory and non-statutory) to which a copy of the ES has been sent. The public must be provided with an opportunity to comment and any views expressed must be taken into account. The LPA should make a copy of the ES freely available for inspection and the developer should make copies available for purchase at a reasonable charge.

The LPA must decide if the ES includes sufficient information to enable the impacts of the proposed project on the environment to be assessed; this is necessary for both outline and detailed planning applications. The LPA can require further information to be provided, or evidence to substantiate that information in the ES. Clearly, this will delay decision making; the principle has been confirmed through UK case law *R. v. Rochdale MBC*.

There is no formal requirement for an LPA to review an ES. However, the review process does provide a systematic and transparent way of evaluating if the environmental information is sufficient to reach a decision. The review may be carried out by the LPA or by independent consultants or IEMA. Such an approach is also useful for those LPAs with limited experience of ESs or those with limited resources to handle a number of applications. The LPA must reach a decision within 16 weeks (not 8 weeks as for other applications) from date of receipt of the ES, unless the developer agrees to a longer period. The LPA must consider the views of the general public and the statutory consultees. Planning conditions and/or obligations may be used to ensure implementation of mitigation and monitoring commitments. Many LPAs have limited resources to enforce implementation and a commitment to an EMS by the developer and/or contractor indicates self-regulation and environmental responsibility.

Appeals and call-ins are the same for planning applications whether the EIA Regulations apply or not; the developer has the right of appeal to the Secretary of State against an adverse decision or against a failure to determine within the time period. The Secretary of State may call-in the application or request a developer to provide further information. The LPA must publish its decision with the main reasons and considerations and a description of the main mitigation measures in the local press.

guiding principle

Close liaison between interested parties throughout the EIA process should minimize the risk of the need for further information post ES submission.

Key fact

The LPA cannot rule that an application is invalid because it considers that the ES does not include sufficient information to assess the environmental impacts. It can, however, refuse the application if there is not enough information to assess the effects.

Chapter 3

Environmental Topics

Each element of the environment likely to be affected by development is considered in a similar way — responsibilities, standards and legislation, the methodology including baseline studies, potential effects, assessment and significance of impacts, mitigation, further guidance and information. Each section is designed to be self-contained. The environmental topics are listed as presented in the Regulations. Interactions between topics and sustainability are drawn together in the final section.

3.1 Introduction

This chapter looks at each element of *'the environment'* recognized by the European Directive as likely to be affected by development and provides guidance on the possible approaches to impact assessment on each in turn. Such work should only be carried out by experienced and qualified assessors in the relevant field and with membership of an appropriate professional body.

This chapter aims to introduce specialist environmental topics to:

- local authority planners and other regulators
- developers/investors and their advisors
- the community and special interest groups
- specialists within the environmental impact assessment (EIA) team to understand each others' approach
- students of specialist topics to understand how their specialism fits into EIA
- provide a quick and easy reference for the EIA co-ordinator.

These introductions provide no more than an overview of the topics, however, the reader is guided to more detailed information and guidance throughout; relevant organizations, sources of information and publications are also detailed in the appendices.

The environmental topics are presented separately since there is specific legislation, guidance and standards applicable to each. Similarly, each topic has characteristic methods and timescales of study, including surveys, and assessment of impacts and significance. Nonetheless, the interactions between environmental issues is a requirement of the EIA Regulations and this is discussed in Section 3.12.

The inter-relationships between environmental factors are also recognized by other legislation which operates in parallel with EIA for the most complex and potentially polluting industries: the Integrated Pollution Prevention and Control (IPPC) regime requires environmental

Contents

Key facts

PPC Regulations require emissions to air, land and water to be considered together to achieve a high level of protection for the environment as a whole.

PPG 3 Planning and Pollution Control advises that EIA and other regulatory requirements such as IPPC should be carried out at the same time

Links

Social Impact Assessment (SIA)

Health Impact Assessment (HIA)

Cumulative Effects Assessment (CEA)

Sustainability Appraisal (SA)

Environmental Risk Assessment (ERA)

assessment of best available techniques (BAT) including:

- consumption and nature of raw materials
- energy efficiency
- waste issues
- accidents and risk
- site restoration.

Sustainable development (SD) has become enshrined within the UK planning system. SD aims to 'balance' or integrate environmental, social and economic issues, thus recognizing the inter-relationships between the environment and socio-economic factors. Accordingly, sustainability and EIA is discussed within considerations of interactions in Section 3.12.

3.2 Population

Introduction

The 1999 European Directive refers to *'population'* in terms of an aspect of the environment that may be affected by the development (the 1985 Directive had used the term *'human beings'*). However, Article 3 of the 1999 Directive still refers to the effects on human beings. Annex III of the Directive, which describes selection criteria for determining the need for EIA, refers to *'the environmental sensitivity of geographical areas … in particular the absorption capacity of the natural environment … [including] (g) densely populated areas'*.

The Guide to Procedures (DETR 2000) – Checklist of matters to be considered for inclusion in an environmental statement, includes the following:

Information describing the project
Numbers to be employed and where they will come from.

Information describing the site and its environment
Population – proximity and numbers.

Assessment of effects on human beings
Change in population arising from the development, and consequential environmental effects (this also refers to visual effects, effects of emissions, effects of noise, effects on transport).

Discussion

It may be understood from this that the 1999 Directive is mostly concerned with *demographic changes* rather than socio-economic or health effects: this is indicated by the change from the use of *'human beings'* to *'population'*. This section therefore focuses on population. However, major developments clearly have the capacity to affect or displace communities, the study of which is generally known as social impact assessment (SIA). This area of expertise, which is often also linked with health impact assessment (HIA) and environmental health impact assessment (EHIA) has grown in recent years in parallel with EIA.

For the purposes of this guide we regard SIA as a separate topic outwith EIA. Nevertheless, it is clearly an issue which should be of principal concern to planning authorities and regulators who may well wish to see such appropriate studies commissioned or reported separately with respect to a development proposal. It is then the role of these authorities – or the inspector at public inquiry – to make judgements balancing the relative effects of development on communities and the natural or heritage environment. Having said this, if a proposed development is likely to have an effect on the health of a community then that is clearly an issue to be addressed in the EIA (see below). The BMA has recommended that an EIA should be judged inadequate unless it shows that the implications for occupational and public health have been addressed.

Town and Country Planning Acts focused on and emphasized social issues before the concept of *'environment'* was introduced and some may contend that to amalgamate the two areas would be a retrograde step; others would urge for an overall assessment so that all impacts can be identified and the development prepared and its cumulative effects assessed as a whole – a step towards assessing the sustainability of a proposal.

Regulators and Consultees

The Health and Safety Executive (HSE) notify local planning authorities of areas which contain toxic, highly reactive, explosive or inflammable substances. They will be consulted by the planning authority on any development proposal which is likely to result in a material increase in the number of persons living, working within, or visiting such a notified area.

The key consultees, however, are the planners and Environmental Health Officers (EHOs) in the local authority. Other consultees may include the emergency services and port health authorities.

Potential Effects

A new development in less populated areas may have beneficial as well as negative effects. The development may stem the outward migration of the population providing new life to the local economy and community; alternatively, the influx of newcomers or those with special skills not available locally may lead to conflict of interest and potential community strains. Certain development types, e.g. reservoirs, may result in the involuntary displacement of communities or individuals on a temporary or permanent basis. On the other hand, they could also provide community benefits in the form of fishing and other forms of recreation or enterprise. It is important to be able to identify the relationship between anticipated population levels and those existing, the timescale over which the changes will take place, and the ability of the existing infrastructure to absorb such changes. Other effects will include potential dominance, coalescence or severance of settlements and communities and effects on property values.

Elements of proposed developments that may have an effect on the health of members of the community – especially those sick or infirm, should be addressed in an EIA. However, they are notoriously difficult to

> *DETR and DOH must ensure that the development of an integrated environmental health impact assessment process is included as part of the UK National Environmental Health Action Plan*
>
> – BMA 1998

Further information

Vanclay F, 1999 *Social Impact Assessment* in Petts, Handbook of EIA

BMA 1998 *Health and Environmental Impact Assessment*

Department of Health 1998 *Saving Lives – Our Healthier Nation*

Key legislation

■ Control of Substances Hazardous to Health Regulations 1999

■ Control of Major Accident Hazards Regulations 1999

case example

Port Health Authority

For a proposed new treated discharge to an estuary, the Port Health Authority took a particular interest in the effects of the discharge on shell fisheries and recreation.

Population

predict since health changes can be caused by a variety of (often pre-existing), conditions and changes may be very small. Links between environmental change and health are also difficult to confirm or qualify. There is frequently a fear of the unknown and a perceived risk – which is difficult to disprove and which those opposed to a scheme may exploit to gather support for their opposition.

The most effective approach is to consider local environmental quality standards – which are designed to protect environmental health – and to estimate if changes will cause these levels to be exceeded.

It is important to recognize the interaction between effects when addressing population issues: issues such as air, noise and landscape, in particular, may have effects on the community – not always of a negative nature.

Methodology

Baseline Studies

Data will be required on the characteristics and trends of the local population in terms of age, sex, marital status, socio-economic status, skills, and vulnerable or sensitive members of the community.

Data will also be required on existing infrastructure (in the case of outward migration, this will be required for the relocation area), housing and property values; schools; hospitals; services (water, gas, electricity, sewerage, telecommunications); transport provision and parking; shops and other commercial needs, e.g. banks, garages; and entertainment.

The Highways Agency (2000) Guidance on Methodology for Multi-Modal Studies (GOMMMS), for example, requires community facilities to be addressed. Footpaths, rights of way and other recreational facilities should be identified and considered. However, views from footpaths are strictly a landscape issue – see Section 3.10.

The environmental boundaries for these baseline studies are clearly going to vary. While they will best be agreed with the local planning authority, individual catchments may include travel-to-work times, health trust area, education areas, etc. Consultation by means of questionnaires or notices in local journals may be most effective at estimating these boundaries.

Project Proposals

These must describe or estimate the potential for population immigration. This will be related to the various phases of the development, i.e. construction, operation/occupation and restoration (where applicable), and how much the needs of the development can be met from the indigenous population. Secondary effects of others being drawn to the area to provide support services also need to be considered. In most instances local communities will be concerned to ensure that they are able to benefit from new employment opportunities and the developer or local agencies may seek to provide training if the working population does not already possess the necessary skills. If this assessment predicts a population increase, its mix (see above) and relative requirements must be estimated.

Impact Prediction and Significance

From the above, the demand for services and infrastructure over and above those existing can be estimated. The scale of differences will indicate the significance of the effects in terms of percentage change over time. It is important to remember that some changes will potentially take many years to become apparent. It is also important to take into consideration variations in culture which may be implied by immigration into a locality. If new housing on a large scale is required, this indirect impact will clearly need detailed assessment in terms of land allocation and environmental impacts.

Mitigation

If significant change is predicted as a result of the proposals it is essential that new provisions or changes are planned, managed and provided for. New employment opportunities should be offered to the local community in the first instance so as not to increase the strain or pressures on existing services, e.g. transport, housing. Mitigation can take the form of strategic alternatives, design or operation. For reasons referred to above, monitoring of effects and implementation of mitigation strategies is essential for social issues.

Sources of Information

Type	*Source*
Demographic data	Office of Population and Census Surveys, local planning authority
Housing stock	Housing department, (local planning authority) estate agents
Infrastructure	Utility undertakers
Commercial facilities	Chambers of Commerce, Economic Development Department, (local planning authority)
Education	Education department, (local planning authority)
Health provision	National Health Trust
Health and safety	Health and Safety Executive
Emergency services	Police, fire, coastguards, Mines Inspectorate
Environmental standards	Environmental Health Department, (local planning authority), Environment Agency

---

Key Features

- Population is concerned with demographic changes and consequential environmental effects (visual, emissions, noise, transport, etc.).
- SIA is a specialist study beyond the scope of EIA.

■ (Environmental) health impact assessment ((E)HIA) and environmental risk assessment are closely related studies.

■ Early and continued consultation is needed to allay fear of the unknown from local communities.

3.3 Transport

Introduction

Although not specifically mentioned as a topic for assessment in the EIA Regulations, road traffic is included as a major issue to be taken into account in determining whether EIA is required for infrastructure, urban development and other projects.

Recent government guidance requires a wider consideration of the implications of development for accessibility by all modes of transport. This section therefore focuses on the assessment in EIA of the effects of development on road traffic, public transport, cycling and walking. Transport developments themselves are discussed separately in Section 4.8; much of what follows is relevant to the impacts of traffic introduced along new roads, and new transport infrastructure which may be required due to increases in travel demand from a development.

Discussion

There is now widespread acceptance of the need to reduce car use for a range of environmental, economic and health reasons. Government Planning Policy Guidance (PPG) now aims to ensure that local authorities guide development to locations where the need to travel by car will be minimized, and where it is easier for people to access jobs, shopping and leisure facilities by public transport, cycling and walking.

Various initiatives have been launched to attempt to reduce traffic levels, including Safer Routes to Schools, and Local Transport Plans for local authorities and Travel Plans (formerly known as green transport plans) for employers. The Sustainable Distribution Strategy (1999) aims to promote the movement of freight by rail and water. A National Waterways Strategy also promotes the use of navigable rivers and canals for passenger and freight transport.

Traffic, and associated effects of air quality and noise, are often the key concerns of residents in areas surrounding a development site. Development can also have implications for access to and use of navigable waterways, public rights of way, for shipping and aircraft, and these need to be taken into account where relevant.

Since the 1980s, it has become common practice, although not a statutory requirement, for Highway Authorities to require major developments to undergo a Traffic Impact Assessment (TIA). Guidelines for TIA should be taken account of for EIA. TIA reports still tend to mainly concentrate on assessing the capacity of the road network to accommodate the increased traffic flows arising from a development, with the assessment of the significance of the changes in traffic and the secondary environmental

---

The EIA Guide to the Procedures recommends that ESs include:

■ a description of the proposed transport and access arrangements for a project

■ an assessment of the effects of the development on local roads and transport

■ assessment of the effects from traffic (road, rail, water, air) related to the development

– DETR 2000

Objectives to integrate planning and transport:

■ to promote more sustainable transport choices for both people and for moving freight

■ to promote accessibility to jobs, shopping, leisure facilities and services by public transport, walking and cycling

■ to reduce the need to travel, especially by car

– PPG 13 2001

Key fact

The generation of travel demand and traffic from a development project and the resultant environmental effects can often be one of the major issues for EIA

"

We need to improve public transport and reduce dependence on the car. The main aim of this White Paper is to increase personal choice by improving the alternatives ...

– DETR 1998

A New Deal for Transport

"

effects being given much less attention. However, good practice in TIA has also extended the assessment to include the accessibility of developments by other modes of travel.

PPG 13 specifically requires the preparation and submission (with the planning application) of Transport Assessments (TAs) for all developments having significant transport implications. The need for a TA depends on the likely significance of environmental effects, the size, scale and location of development. For small schemes, the TA should simply outline the transport aspects of the application. For major proposals, the assessment should illustrate accessibility to the site by all modes, measures to improve access by public transport, walking and cycling, and reduce the need for parking. Where appropriate a Travel Plan should be included.

Regulators and Consultees

Developers should hold early discussions with the local transport/highway authority (county councils or unitary authorities) in order to clarify the need for and scope of a TA. The local planning authority should be consulted on the scope of assessments for secondary impacts including noise and air quality. The Highways Agency should be consulted where a development may have implications for motorways and trunk roads. Where public rights of way are potentially affected, the local highway authority, and where relevant, the Ramblers Association, British Horse Society and other local user groups, should also be consulted.

Public transport operators and authorities will be important consultees where their operations are potentially affected, both to provide information on existing services, and to identify potential new or improved services to serve a proposed development. Sustrans should also be consulted where a National Cycle Network route is potentially affected.

British Waterways should be consulted on developments affecting navigable waterways where it is the navigation authority, and the Environment Agency (EA) is a statutory consultee for developments affecting the banks or bed of a river or stream. The Civil Aviation Authority is also a statutory consultee on development near airports; they have specific safety requirements relating to building heights and areas of open water that could attract birds. Similarly, port authorities should be consulted on development proposals affecting their interests.

Potential Effects

Developments can have a wide range of effects relating to traffic and transport, depending on the type, location and scale of development, and types of traffic likely to be generated. New travel demand can be generated, or diverted on to different routes, and this can take the form of cars or heavy vehicles, buses, cyclists and pedestrians attracted to a site.

Impacts are likely to vary during construction, operational and decommissioning phases. Construction works commonly require a range of light and heavy vehicles (including abnormal loads) to access a site from the main trunk road network. Certain types of development are by nature

---

guiding principle

The scope of the TIA must consider the scope of the air quality and noise impact assessments

Key fact

Traffic Impact Assessment (TIA) guides planning conditions, obligations and any required financial contributions

Regulators and consultees

Local Transport Authorities (County Councils)

Highways Agency

DTLR

Public transport operators

Navigation authorities

Civil Aviation Authority

Port authorities

Sustrans, Ramblers Association, British Horse Society, local groups

Transport 2000

British Waterways

Environment Agency

Living Streets

Links

Noise and Air Quality

Health Impact Assessment

Cumulative Effects Assessment

Energy Use and Climate Change

Transport

case example

Inner City Regeneration

Proposals for a major redevelopment of derelict and underused land involved the creation of a new mixed use local centre as well as the diversion of high levels of traffic away from existing residential streets. This required the preparation of a Traffic Impact Assessment, which assessed the effects of development traffic and traffic diversions on the capacity of local road junctions, as well as the potential for new bus routes to serve the development to increase public transport accessibility. A study was carried out of the potential to improve the existing pedestrian and cycle links from surrounding areas which would link up with the surrounding bus, underground and rail services. The ES also identified wider potential effects of traffic on noise, air quality, pedestrian amenity, and severance, and mitigation measures were proposed. The ES therefore integrated a range of assessments to identify and mitigate the transport impacts of the development.

guiding principle

Early and continued liaison between traffic, air quality, noise consultants and the EIA co-ordinator are vital

considered to be large generators of personal travel, e.g. offices, shops and leisure facilities, with housing the start and end of most trips. Business parks and industrial estates tend to involve a large proportion of freight deliveries. Mixed developments may reduce travel demand by enabling multi-purpose trips to be made, whereas retail and leisure developments can lead to distinct peaks in traffic. The timing of travel demand will also help determine the mode of travel and impacts of traffic movements on the surrounding area, e.g. if during rush-hours or quieter night-time periods.

The location and accessibility of a development will determine the mode of that travel, e.g. retail developments in areas without frequent bus services and good pedestrian and cycling access will lead to an increase in car travel. Conversely, insensitive development can disrupt pedestrian and cycle routes and discourage the use of public transport. Developments can enhance or reduce the accessibility to the disabled. Increases in traffic generated by a development can lead to increased noise and vibration in the vicinity of roads affected, to increase in local and regional air pollution, and to an increase in energy use and contributions to global greenhouse gas emissions. See Sections 3.4 and 3.8.

Increased motor vehicle traffic can conflict with the use of a route by pedestrians, cyclists and horse-riders, and cause increased danger, fear, accidents and delays. The danger from traffic can contribute to 'severance' of roadside communities from facilities and places they use by reducing the number of road crossings people make. Conversely, the redistribution of traffic brought about by the creation of new streets or bypasses can lead to reduced traffic impacts through residential areas, although impacts may still be created elsewhere. Increased traffic can also lead to increased wildlife losses through road casualties, particularly where migration routes are affected.

Methodology

Baseline Studies

The assessment of the traffic and travel impacts of a development requires a wide range of information on the existing transport network and any proposed changes. Baseline information can comprise the levels and composition of traffic, the character of the road network, road safety and accident levels, public transport services and use, cycling and pedestrian movements and facilities, as well as the levels of severance, pedestrian delay, noise and air pollution, dust and dirt created by existing traffic levels. Baseline conditions also include future planned changes to existing conditions that are unrelated to the proposed development.

Local transport authorities possess a range of data on existing traffic levels and composition (including heavy goods vehicles (HGVs)), traffic growth, trends, congestion, car parking and road accidents. Traffic data may be available by hour, several hours or daily average; the peak hours of travel are of most interest. The Highways Agency hold relevant automated traffic count data for trunk roads. The DTLR holds national traffic count data and publishes traffic growth trends as the National Road Traffic Forecasts.

The location of land uses sensitive to increases in traffic should be identified, including schools, hospitals, dwellings, and areas of importance for outdoor recreation, heritage, landscape and nature conservation. Local planning authorities will hold information on the other major developments in the area that have received planning permission.

Public transport operators hold relevant information on local service routes, timetables and their use by passengers, as well as any current proposals for new and improved services. Information on the location, standard and use of cycle and pedestrian routes should be available from local authorities, Sustrans, the Ramblers Association, and local cycling and pedestrian groups. Information on the modes of travel used in the area will be available from the latest National Transport Survey published by the government, in London by the latest London Area Transport Survey, more local census data, and any more recent local authority surveys.

A review of existing data will determine the need for any new classified road user surveys along road sections or at junctions by type of vehicles, pedestrians and cyclists, at different times of the day. The location and condition of pedestrian routes and road crossings, cycling conditions, public transport facilities and services and land uses people need to walk and cycle to, should also be determined. Assessing the existing operation of the highway network requires traffic count data showing the turning movements made at key junctions and links and the junction capacity. Standard assessment models are available from the Transport Research Laboratory (TRL).

Baseline conditions should be identified in relation to the current year, and projected forward to the defined year of development, taking account of any permitted future development that will affect the transport network and traffic levels. Care should be taken in applying past trends to future predictions, as these trends are based on increases in car ownership and socio-economic factors that may not be applicable and may risk double-counting.

Traffic levels are usually defined in terms of the annual average daily flow and hourly flows during defined peak periods. The data needed for related assessments of air quality and noise should be identified at an early stage. Information on traffic levels during non-peak periods may also be required to assess environmental impacts during other sensitive times.

Project Proposals

The transportation elements of the design and management of development proposals, both on- and off-site, should be identified and described in an Environmental Statement (ES). Information, which should be as accurate as possible, is needed on the nature, size and location of the development to determine the likely generation of travel and the modes likely to be used. This includes the intended mix, size and phasing of proposed land uses, numbers of intended residents, employees and expected visitors, hours of opening and working, access arrangements including service access, and the types of traffic anticipated.

The physical transportation infrastructure proposed for highways, public transport, cycling and pedestrian movement should be fully described. Site access points to the existing network should be identified for all

Relevant plans for consultation:
- Regional Transport Assessments
- Structure and Local Plans
- Transport Plan and Programme
- Local Transport Plans
- Cycling and Walking Strategies
- Road Traffic Reduction Reports
- Travel Plans

case example

Mixed-use Urban Regeneration
EIA specialists were brought into the team at a late stage of the project. TIA studies were well advanced. Additional surveys had to be carried out to provide traffic data for air quality and noise assessments. If these had been considered earlier in the project, overall costs to the developer would have been reduced.

modes of travel. Levels of car parking on a site can heavily influence people's choice of travel mode.

Information on types and numbers of construction vehicles, any abnormal loads, their routing and timing of access, is generally required for EIA, as well as any requirements for demolition, site clearance, delivery of plant and construction materials, and removal of wastes.

Predicting the generated travel likely to arise from a new development comprises different elements:

- the calculation of travel generation
- the assignment of travel between different routes
- the assignment of travel between different modes.

Trip generation forecasts from a development can be derived from statistical packages that use the type, size and location of development to generate daily and hourly car trip rates. There are a range of statistical packages; the Trip Rate Information Computer System (TRICS) database is commonly used.

New roads and motorways:

The New Approach to Appraisal (NATA)

■ An Appraisal Summary Table
  Environment
  Safety
  Economy
  Accessibility
  Integration

■ The achievement of local and regional objectives

■ Options to
  resolve problems
  consultation
  audit

■ Supporting Analyses
  distribution and equity
  affordability and financial sustainability
  practicality
  public acceptability

– DETR 2000

The likely origin and destination of trips can be predicted by models that require information on local population and land use, and the known or estimated origins and destinations of customers, employees, visitors and delivery vehicles. The types of trips generated may include a mixture of new trips or trips diverted from elsewhere (e.g. from a new competing supermarket), primary trips (where the development is the only destination), and linked trips with multiple destinations. Assigning the predicted (multi-modal) trips from a development between actual routes in the area can then be made by using the known conditions on the local transport network.

Impact Prediction and Significance

The scope and methodology behind the assessment of impacts should be discussed and agreed with the local transport authority and/or Highways Agency as appropriate. The assessment should identify the magnitude of the impacts, who is affected, and whether the impact is significant. The affected groups should be identified in relation to sensitive groups (such as children, elderly or disabled people, vulnerable road users) and land uses (e.g. hospitals, schools, dwellings, visitor attractions, and areas of landscape/townscape, historical, nature conservation or recreational importance).

The extent of the study area should be defined as the areas likely to be significantly affected; this is defined in Institution of Highways and Transportation (IHT) guidance as roads with greater than 10% increase in traffic (as traffic on an uncongested road generally varies by up to 10% on a day-to-day basis), although lower increases of 5% may be significant for congested routes. IEA guidance recommends a detailed assessment of the environmental effects where total or HGV traffic increases by over 30% or by 10% in sensitive areas.

The accessibility of the site for the relevant range of travel modes should be assessed in the light of the distance and linkages to existing and proposed public transport services, the quality of pedestrian and cycle routes, and any adopted local authority standards for accessibility. The modes of travel likely to be used for trips to and from the site should be assessed, based on the nature of the development, information on the site accessibility via a range of modes, the derived car trip rates, and the existing modal split.

The capacity of existing road junctions to accommodate the predicted future levels of traffic with the development is likely to be of concern for trip generating development. A range of standard assessment models applicable to assessing driver delay and junction capacity in different systems of junctions are available from the TRL.

The impacts on environmental conditions along a road should first be assessed in terms of the percentage changes in traffic levels in the different time periods modelled. The modelling procedures and changes in data between different stages should be clarified to avoid confusion. If road traffic levels in any phase are predicted to be increased by more than 10% on the surrounding network, detailed assessments of the traffic impacts on air quality, noise and vibration may be required in accordance with IEA guidance (see Sections 3.4 and 3.8).

The impacts of traffic arising from the development should also be assessed in areas affected for all phases, in relation to community severance, road safety and visual intrusion. Associated with severance are pedestrian delay, fear and intimidation. The safety implications of development for all modes of travel should be considered from an early stage.

For the construction phase, the likely effects of the increased heavy vehicle traffic, albeit temporary, along routes between the development site and the trunk road network should be assessed in the light of the suitability to accept such traffic and the potential impacts on sensitive receptors as discussed above.

Mitigation

Planning conditions and obligations can be used by local planning authorities to require mitigation measures for transport to be implemented and this includes the provision of facilities for pedestrians, cyclists and public transport users.

The highest form of mitigation for transport is to minimize the need to travel in terms of trips made and distance travelled, through locating the source and destination of a trip close to each other. Where a development is predicted to generate significant new trips by car, locating in areas with good levels of access to public transport, cycling and walking will go some way to reducing potential increases in traffic, and the assessment should consider how alternative modes of travel to the car can be promoted.

Public transport provision to a development site can be improved through discussions with the relevant operators, who may support the development through improved or new services. The potential for services to link the site with high standards of existing provision nearby, and for the provision of new forms of travel, e.g. a light rail route along a former railway line, should be investigated where relevant.

Key fact

It is **the degree of change** with the development, as well as the absolute levels of traffic arising, that should be assessed for EIA

The environmental effects of traffic changes along a road should be assessed in relation to the times of day where **the greatest degree of change** in traffic levels are predicted to arise, and in light of **the sensitivity of receptors** to the traffic rather than solely during the peak traffic hours

– IEA 1993

Transport

Cycling can be promoted through provision of a cycle path network linking to existing routes, cycle parking and shower/changing areas. Access on foot can be promoted to a site through safe and high-standard footpaths which link the development to existing housing, services and public transport facilities.

Accommodating the extra traffic from the development through increased road capacity is now considered to contribute to general traffic growth, and so may be counter-productive to efforts to minimize car traffic from a development.

Traffic management and 'traffic calming' schemes may be required to ensure that traffic flows are restricted to routes capable of accommodating them without significant environmental and safety impacts. This may include pavement widening and road narrowing, suitable surfacing treatments, provision of street furniture, lighting and signing, rumble devices, traffic islands, 'raised tables' and speed bumps. Management measures include reducing speed limits around sensitive areas such as schools and housing. 'Home Zones' are likely to be designated in the future by local authorities as areas where the design of streets is specifically geared to allowing a range of road uses through intensive traffic calming and reduced speed limits. Traffic management should be integrated into development site design, where relevant.

Minimizing car parking provision for a development can limit the generation of car trips, particularly in areas with congestion or parking problems, where alternative modes of travel are available.

Developments requiring movements for freight require good access to the trunk road network, and should avoid using congested and residential routes for freight movements. Consideration should be given to the use of rail freight, water-borne transport and pipelines.

The impacts of heavy goods vehicles accessing a site during construction and operational phases can be mitigated through defining suitable routes to be used that avoid sensitive roadside properties and receptors, avoid travelling during sensitive times of day (e.g. rush-hours in congested areas, school opening and closing times, or late at night), and ensuring that the agreed routes are complied with. Commitments should be made in the ES to required routes for construction traffic.

case examples

Several 'car-free' housing developments, have required residents to state that they will not own a car.

Commercial/industrial businesses have put bus passes in employees' wage packets to reduce car travel.

The National Trust's Prior Park landscape garden outside Bath provides no car parking while advising visitors to use the bus instead.

case example

The stone for repairs to Windsor Castle was transported from Bath along the Kennet and Avon Canal.

Sources of Information	
Type	*Source*
Traffic data	Local authorities, Highways Agency, DTLR
Public transport data	Operators
Local transport plans	Local authorities
Travel plans	Local employers
Cycle and pedestrian routes	Sustrans, Ramblers Association, Local groups, Living Streets

| Boat/ship data | British Waterways, Boatowners Association, Port and Harbour authorities |
| Aircraft data | Civil Aviation Authority, Local airports |

Key Features

- Traffic effects are associated with most types of development and are often contentious.

- The impacts of travel demand and traffic generation are often one of the key issues for an EIA.

- TIA has traditionally been required by highway authorities for major trip-generating development; TAs are now required by PPG 13 for development with significant transport.

- Good practice guidance requires assessment of the secondary environmental effects of road traffic and the potential effects on other modes of transport. Close liaison is needed with air quality and noise specialists.

- TAs should assess the accessibility to the site by all modes, the likely modal split of journeys to and from the site, and measures proposed to mitigate transport impacts, improve access by public transport, walking and cycling, to reduce the need for parking, including Travel Plans.

- EIA should identify the significance of the effects of travel demand on sensitive receptors, as well as the ability of the road network to accommodate the increased volume of traffic.

- The prediction of trips generated by a new development has traditionally focused solely on car travel, but new guidance is being developed to extend this to trips made by public transport, walking and cycling.

- The design requirements for accommodating the requirements of different modes of travel, including bus routes and traffic calming, should be identified and incorporated into developments at an early stage. Measures should be incorporated into a development proposal to mitigate for the significant effects of development in relation to all travel modes.

- Government guidance aims to reduce dependence on the car.

Key legislation and guidance

Transport Act 2000

PPG 13: Transport 2001

DETR 1998. Transport White Paper – A New Deal for Transport

DETR 2001. Transport 2010: The 10 Year Plan

DETR. Places, Streets and Movement

DETR/CABE 2000. By Design – Urban Design in the Planning System

DETR 2000. Road Safety Strategy – Tomorrow's Roads – Safer for Everyone

DETR 1999. Sustainable Distribution Strategy

Institute of Environmental Assessment 1993. Guidelines for the Environmental Assessment of Road Traffic

Institution of Highways and Transportation 1994. Guidelines for Traffic Impact Assessment

Highways Agency 1993. Design Manual for Roads and Bridges Volume 11: Environmental Assessment

DETR 2000. Guidance on the Methodology for Multi-Modal Studies (GOMMMS)

DETR 2000. A Good Practice Guide for the Development of Local Transport Plans

"

Planning authorities should: seek to reduce car dependence by facilitating more walking and cycling, by improving linkages by public transport between housing, jobs, local services and local amenity and by planning for mixed use

– PPG 3 2000
"

3.4   Noise and Vibration

Introduction

There are many sounds detectable by the human ear that bring pleasure: the sound of laughter, birds singing and music. There are also numerous other sounds that cause annoyance: the sound of a pneumatic drill, heavy traffic, a car alarm or music breaking out at 2 a.m. These unwanted sounds are referred to as noise. There are few developments that do not give rise to noise impacts at some stage. As a result, the EIA Regulations

"

Noise is defined as unwanted sound
"

Noise and Vibration

Key fact

Noise is the largest single cause of complaint to local authorities

require noise and vibration emissions from developments to be described, together with resultant noise levels and their effects.

Noise Terms and Concepts

- *Sound* consists of pressure variations in the air detectable by the human ear. The unit of measurement of sound pressure is the decibel (dB). Pressure variations have two characteristics, frequency and amplitude.

- Sound *frequency* is heard as pitch or tone. It is the speed of pressure variation in the air measured in Hz (cycles per second). The range audible to humans is approximately 20–18,000 Hz, however, sensitivity is usually within the 500–5000 Hz range important in speech communication.

- Sound *amplitude* is heard as volume or loudness. It is the excess of pressure over the local atmospheric mean at any instance. It can be measured as a sound power, intensity or pressure.

- Sound *power* is an inherent property of a machine or process. A compressor or a jet engine at a certain throttle or load setting generates a certain amount of sound energy, irrespective of environmental factors. Sound power level is usually measured in decibels relative to a standard.

- Sound *intensity* is the amount of sound energy passing through a unit area. Measurement is technically difficult and is rarely used in environmental noise assessment.

- Sound *pressure* is the instantaneous excess of pressure over mean atmospheric pressure caused by the passing of a wave of sound energy – influenced by intervening environmental variables. Sound pressure level is usually measured in decibels relative to a standard.

Terms Used in EIA

- In EIA it is important to determine the loudness experienced by people rather than the physical magnitude of the sound. The human ear is not equally sensitive to sound at all frequencies. In order to make sound measurement comparable to the sensitivity of the ear, the reduction in sensitivity to high and to low frequencies has to be introduced by weighting. The commonly applied weighting is A-weighting, and is internationally standardized.

- A-weighted sound pressure levels in the natural and built environment range between 0 and about 140 dB. Because the scale is logarithmic, decibels do not add and subtract arithmetically. A doubling or halving of sound pressure equates with a 3 dB increase or reduction in level.

- The sound level terms most commonly used in EIA are
  - the $L_{A10,t}$ is the level exceeded for 10% of the measurement period, it is an indicator of the noisier events and is most often used to characterize road traffic noise
  - the $L_{A90,t}$ is the level exceeded for 90% of the measurement period, it is an indicator of the underlying tranquility behind event noise and is used to characterize the background noise in an environment

- the L_{Amax}, is the instantaneous maximum level and has no time dimension
- the $L_{Aeq,t}$, is an all-encompassing measure describing all of the noise in an environment, both steadily in the background and occurring in transient events; it is a description of the ambient noise level.

This section focuses on noise; vibration is less commonly a significant issue in EIA, though it is an important factor in some circumstances such as piling in construction, blasting, soil compaction and rail and road traffic. It may be a major issue with regard to protected buildings and assessment of cultural heritage effects. The measurement and assessment of environmental vibration should be undertaken by experienced specialists.

Discussion

Noise assessment to date has generally been carried out on a project-by-project basis, with the impact of a proposed development being assessed and mitigation measures proposed. However, little attention has been paid to the cumulative effects of environmental noise, that is noise generated by human activity from road traffic, railways, air transport, industry, recreation and transport. Noise is a growing problem and needs to be dealt with in a more holistic manner.

In recognition of the need to tackle noise pollution, the European Union (EU) has proposed a Directive 'relating to the Assessment and Management of Environmental Noise'. Member States will then have responsibility for developing their own methods and approaches to limit setting, noise mapping, action plans, providing information to the public and developing additional indicators. Within the UK, the Department for Environment, Food and Rural Affairs (DEFRA) is engaged on a proposed National Ambient Noise Strategy.

Clearly, all of these initiatives will have implications for noise impact assessment within EIA, potentially affecting the way noise assessments are carried out and the standards that are worked to. The noise impacts of an individual project will be able to be examined within the wider context of an area and noise abatement measures considered as part of wider strategies.

Regulators and Consultees

For noise impact assessments, the Local EHO should be the principal point of contact. EHOs should be able to provide advice about key concerns or issues within the local area. They can also advise on the approach to the assessment, such as monitoring locations and potentially sensitive receptors, the noise indices to consider (e.g. L_{Aeq}, L_{A10}) and the time periods over which baseline noise monitoring and impact predictions should be made.

> *The growth in noise pollution is unsustainable because it involves direct, as well as cumulative, adverse health effects. It also adversely affects future generations, and has socio-cultural, aesthetic and economic effects*
>
> – WHO 1999

Draft EU Directive

The introduction of common indicators, computation methods and measurement methods for noise exposure, monitoring of noise pollution in the EU and the development of an EU strategy to improve the situation, exchange of information, and legislation on noise emission

Regulators and consultees

Local Authority Environmental Health Department

Noise and Vibration

Key fact

A change of 3 dB in a steady noise is the smallest perceptible under normal conditions and a change of 10 dB corresponds with a doubling or halving of perceived loudness. The level of an intermittent noise changes as the number of events in a certain time varies, a doubling or halving in the number of events produces a change of 3 dB in level. A change of 1 dB is perceptible in an intermittent noise level because the perception of noisiness is a compound both of the noise level of each event and of the frequency of the events

Between 5% and 15% of the EU population suffers serious noise induced sleep disturbance

Key fact

'Sound measurements have to be carried out over sufficient time to get statistically reliable results'

Depending on the nature of the impacts, other consultees may also need to be consulted. For example, if noise is likely to affect bird populations within a designated area, such as a Site of Special Scientific Interest (SSSI) or Special Protection Area (SPA), then English Nature and others should be consulted. Similarly, if the development is likely to generate levels of vibration that can cause structural damage to historic buildings then English Heritage should be consulted.

Potential Effects

Noise and vibration impacts can arise during all phases of a project. For many developments the most significant noise impacts often arise in the phases leading up to operation. Demolition, site preparation and construction often involve the use of noisy plant and activities such as piling and the transportation of materials by large numbers of heavy goods vehicles. During operation, noisy activities may subside and traffic might become the principal concern. However, industrial, and increasingly commercial and retail developments, might generate noise. Significant sources include air handling machinery providing ventilation, heating and cooling, and sound systems in shops, bars and other entertainment premises. Activities such as mineral extraction can be persistently or intermittently noisy throughout the lifespan of the project.

Noise can lead to annoyance and disturbance such as interference with speech communication and interruption of rest and sleep. At extreme levels it can induce hearing impairment and under some circumstances has been shown to affect physiological and mental health, performance and social behaviour. Noise can disturb wildlife and domestic animals. Ground vibration can provoke annoyance and in extreme cases lead to damage to buildings.

Methodology

Baseline Studies

Baseline noise or vibration survey results may fulfil any of a number of purposes. The baseline conditions might affect the proposed development (e.g. the noise exposure of housing development sites, requiring assessment under PPG 24) so survey data might feed back into the development design process. The proposed development might be a source of noise or vibration and assessment of its impact will involve comparison with the baseline conditions. In the case of road and rail developments the noise impact might trigger statutory compensation and the baseline condition is one of the factors determining eligibility. Each of these purposes might demand a particular approach to the design of the survey.

The baseline studies should identify existing sources of noise in an area and characterize variations in noise over time, e.g. variations between day and night, between weekdays and weekends, or at different times of year, as appropriate: the scope of the studies will depend on the characteristics of the proposed development.

Survey or sample durations should take into account the stability of the noise climate. Where the ambient noise is steady interval samples over a typical day may be sufficient. Where the ambient noise is variable, automatic monitoring over several typical days may be needed. Some sites, such as those close to railways or under flight paths, might exhibit stable, predictable ambient noise levels because of the dominant intermittent source, but variable underlying background noise levels.

While the greatest volumes of traffic resulting from a development may not occur during the night, this may be the time of the greatest noise impact. The noise indices to be measured will also vary, e.g. for roads the L_{A10}, 18 h index is generally used. The locations selected for noise monitoring also need to reflect the position of sensitive receptors and the area of impact, e.g. the study area for a proposed airport will be considerably larger than that for a new residential development. Sensitive receptors include residential areas, schools and hospitals.

Noise monitoring

Baseline noise levels can also be calculated rather than derived from direct measurement. Calculation is possible where the existing environment is dominated by a single noise source, such as traffic, and a recognized methodology, such as the Calculation of Road Traffic Noise (CRTN) is available.

While baseline surveys will establish the existing noise climate of the area, it may also be necessary to project the baseline forward to a future year, such as the proposed year of opening or design year. This may need to take into account anticipated changes in the volume of traffic on nearby roads and other factors that may affect noise levels in the area.

Project Proposals

The description of the project proposals should be sufficient to identify all significant noise and vibration sources and for the level of noise or vibration to be predicted. It should also include the time periods when impacts are likely to arise, e.g. working hours during construction and operation, and a description of the characterstics of the noise.

Noise sources can, for example, give rise to high-pitched noise, low-frequency hums, intermittent or continuous noise. The alleged health effects of low-frequency noise has been a contentious issue for proposed windfarms. The characteristics of the noise are important in determining peoples' reaction to them, i.e. the degree of nuisance they cause. The sound of traffic may become part of the general background noise that a person hears, while reversing alarms on construction vehicles or the sound of a pneumatic drill may be highly irritating. Noise with an information content such as music or speech communication is potentially annoying at any audible level.

---

case example

Proposed Energy Recovery Facility

The ES for this proposal included an assessment of the effects of noise and vibration on over-wintering and resident bird populations. Birds such as lapwing, redshank and black-tailed godwit can react to disturbance by avoiding the area from which noise was emitted.

The proposed ERF is located in close proximity to a SSSI, SPA, cSAC and Ramsar site. The increase in noise during construction was predicted to make the foreshore unattractive for use by the majority of wildfowl and waders for the duration of that activity. Impacts were, however, only considered to be localized and short term.

Key legislation and guidance

Control of Pollution Act 1974

Environmental Protection Act 1990

Noise Act 1996

Noise Insulation Regulations 1975

Noise Insulation Amendment Regulations 1988

BS7445: 1991: Description and measurement of environmental noise

BS6472: 1992: Guide to evaluation of human exposure to vibration in buildings

BS4142: 1997: Method for rating noise affecting mixed residential and industrial areas

BS5228: 1997: Noise and vibration control on construction and open sites

BS8233: 1999: Sound insulation and noise reduction for buildings – Code of Practice

WHO Guidelines on Community Noise (1999)

PPC Regulations 2000

PPG 24 Planning and Noise 1994

Building Regulations

---

case example

Proposed Airport

The Scoping Exercise for a proposed airport identified the following potential noise sources:

- aeroplanes taxiing, taking off, flying overhead and landing
- vehicle movements within the airport
- traffic on surrounding roads
- trains serving the airport; and
- other miscellaneous activities.

Noise and Vibration

Impact Prediction and Significance

The noise or vibration impacts should be assessed at a number of representative sensitive receptors. Worst case conditions should be described with a commentary where appropriate on the risk of their occurring.

A number of standard prediction procedures are defined in relevant legislation and guidelines. These include the methods for the calculation of road traffic and railway noise, and for the prediction of construction noise. Prediction methods for other noise sources such as industrial and commercial installations and processes are not standardized and it is important that the ES reports the method chosen. In all cases the input assumptions should be reported, including *source variables* such as emission factors, traffic flows, times of occurrence and diurnal patterns; and *geographical variables* such as ground cover, topography, meteorological conditions and the presence of permanent barriers; and *receptor variables* such as the heights above ground of the locations for which calculations have been undertaken and whether facade reflections have been included.

An EIA method for evaluating road traffic noise is specified in some detail in the *Design Manual for Roads and Bridges* and aspects of the process can be adopted for other types of project. BS4142 offers a method for evaluating noise from industrial and commercial sources, while various industry-specific guidelines are available for projects such as wind farms.

In the case of residential developments, a noise assessment will not only need to examine the impact of the development on the environment, but also the impact of the surrounding environment on the development.

PPG 24: Planning and Noise introduces the concept of Noise Exposure Categories to help local planning authorities with their consideration of applications for residential development.

When considering the significance of the impact many EIAs only consider the resultant noise levels in relation to standards or guidelines, e.g. BS4142 as it provides a method for assessing the likelihood of complaints. However, 'the likelihood of complaints' depends on a number of factors in addition to the increase in noise levels and these are often overlooked. Additional factors include the sensitivity of the receptor(s), the number of people/area affected and the time and duration of the impact. Noise is often considered more acceptable during the daytime, however, it is not acceptable in the vicinity of schools or hospitals. Noise impact assessments also tend to define night-time as being between 11 p.m. and 7 a.m. However, this overlooks the sleeping patterns of shift-workers and infants.

Predicting vibration impacts is a complex process but models to help do exist. BS7385: Part 2: 1993 'Evaluation and measurement for vibration in buildings' gives guidance on the levels above which building structures could be damaged. Disturbance to people can be assessed in accordance with BS6472: 1992 'Evaluation of human exposure to vibration in buildings'.

Key fact

Traffic noise is likely to be a factor in most development proposals. It is, therefore, important for the noise and traffic consultants to ensure that appropriate data for noise modelling is available early on in the EIA process

Further information

DoT 1988. Calculation of Road Traffic Noise

HMSO 1995, Calculation of Railway Noise

The Working Group on Wind Turbine Noise, The Assessment and Rating of Noise from Wind Farms, 1996. ETSU

Design Manual for Roads and Bridges. Vol.11 Environmental Assessment

Mitigation

Noise impacts can be avoided through careful consideration of the site location, layout and design, the selection of appropriate plant or technology or controls on working hours. Noise reduction measures include fitting silencers to noisy plant, screening off areas where particularly noisy activities are taking place and erecting acoustic bunds or barriers. Compensation measures may include the provision of specific glazing for properties adversely affected by noise from a development.

Establishing good relations with the affected community is an important part of managing noise impacts. Warning of any particularly noisy activities should be provided during both the construction and operation phases. A procedure should be in place to allow people to register their complaints when adverse noise impacts arise, and for these complaints to be responded to (see also Chapter 5).

Vibration infrequently occurs at levels which require mitigation measures to be introduced. However, vibration control measures would include altering construction techniques to avoid piling, or using alternative forms of piling that generate less vibration; where explosives are used, the energy within each explosion could be reduced.

The local planning authority can control noise and vibration using powers under the Control of Pollution Act 1974 or the Environmental Protection Act 1990. Developments may also be carried out under conditional prior consents in accordance with Section 61 of the Control of Pollution Act (Section 61 agreements).

Sources of Information

Type	*Source*
Existing noise survey data and advice on scope of assessment	Local Authority (Environmental Health Department)
Technical advice	Institute of Acoustics
British Standards, e.g. BS4142	British Standards Institute
Tranquil Area Maps	Council for the Protection of Rural England (CPRE)
Briefing and fact sheets	National Society for Clean Air (NSCA)

Key Features

■ Noise and vibration impact assessment is a specialist activity, involving the use of complex calculations and technical terminology. It is, therefore, important to ensure that data is presented as clearly and systematically as possible and that the effects of any increase in noise are clearly explained.

■ Noise and vibration impact assessments should not simply determine whether a given threshold is met, but should explain the actual effects on people, wildlife and buildings.

Biodiversity

■ The assessment of noise and vibration is inter-related with other topics in the ES and close liaison with other EIA team members is required. For example, traffic data may be required to predict noise impacts; noise may affect wildlife; and noise mitigation measures, such as bunds, can have landscape and visual impacts.

3.5   Biodiversity (Fauna and Flora)

Introduction

The EIA Directive and Regulations refer to 'fauna and flora' – the study of these is generically termed ecology. However, of increasing concern is the need to protect 'biodiversity', which relates to the variety of species and habitats.

If biodiversity is likely to be significantly affected by the proposed development, the Regulations require a description of the baseline conditions or state, the likely significant effects and measures envisaged to prevent, reduce or offset such adverse effects.

Discussion

Environmental assessment of ecological issues has particular links with other EU Directives, i.e.

■ the Habitats Directive (92/43/EEC)
■ the Wild Birds Directive (79/409/EEC)

for which 'Appropriate Assessments' are required in accordance with the Conservation (Natural Habitats, etc.) Regulations 1994 (as amended in 2000). Therefore, if a proposed development site is, or is in the vicinity of, a site to be designated as a (candidate) Special Area of Conservation (SAC) in accordance with the Habitats Directive, or as a SPA in accordance with the Birds Directive, then it will save time and effort if the different assessments required are co-ordinated. Advice on the links between EIA and the Habitats Directive are given in PPG 9 Nature Conservation. Appropriate assessments are carried out by the competent authority which in most cases is the Local Planning Authority using data provided by the developer. (The competent authority can also be from other organizations in certain circumstances, e.g. Highways Agency, Ministry of Defence.)

The selection criteria for screening Schedule 2 development draws special attention to the environmental sensitivity of geographical areas likely to be affected by development, having regard to the **absorption capacity of the natural environment** including:

■ wetlands
■ coastal zones
■ mountain and forest areas
■ nature reserves and parks
■ areas classified or protected under Member States' legislation; as well as the Habitats and Wild Birds Directives.

Key legislation and guidance

Habitats Directive (identifies Special Areas of Conservation) 1992

Wild Birds Directive (identifies Special Protection Areas) 1979

PPG 9 Nature Conservation 1994

Wildlife and Countryside Act 1981

Protection of Badgers Act 1992

UK Biodiversity Action Plan

Hedgerows Regulations 1997

Habitats Regulations 1994

Countryside and Rights of Way Act 2000

Biodiversity is the total range of variability among systems and organisms at the following levels of organization:

■ Bioregional
■ Landscape
■ Ecosystem
■ Habitat
■ Communities
■ Species
■ Populations
■ Individuals
■ Genes

and the relationships within and between these levels.

– Byron 2000

Key fact

The Directive on EIA makes it clear that the presence of a cSAC or SPA in the vicinity does not necessarily imply that projects in such areas are automatically to be subject to an assessment under the EIA Directive

---

It is thought that the capacity of the ecological environment has already been exceeded by previous overdevelopment and lack of recognition of the value of the resource. Local authorities may be able to require ecological planning gain and contributions to HAPs and SAPs targets under PPG 9 Nature Conservation.

PPG 3 Housing requires local authorities to give priority to reusing previously developed land within urban areas, in preference to the development of greenfield sites. However, brownfield sites may have significant ecological value due to their lack of disturbance and may not be accessible through sustainable transport; greenfield sites may be ecologically poor due to intensive agricultural practices. The government's requirement for brownfield primacy may cause problems for local authorities with regard to meeting sustainable development and biodiversity objectives.

Regulators and consultees

English Nature will be particularly concerned with the effects of development in or within two kilometres of or likely to affect a SSSI notified in accordance with Section 28 of the Wildlife and Countryside Act 1981. They also hold information on Ramsar sites, National Nature Reserves and Ancient Woodlands. The Environment Agency should be consulted on wetland sites and is the main contact for certain BAP habitats and species. The Wildlife Trusts (local branches of the Royal Society for Nature Conservation) should also be consulted as a matter of course since they often hold local ecological information, especially about sites that are not SSSIs, cSACs or SPAs, e.g. Sites of Interest for Nature Conservation (SINC). Similarly local authorities will hold information on Local Nature Reserves.

Potential Effects

To understand the potential effects of a development it is necessary to understand the likely **changes** and behaviour of any ecological resources and their interactions.

The assessment should cover habitats, species, varieties and ecological processes within the site and its surroundings. Depending on the location of the development, the assessment should address both the terrestrial and freshwater aquatic environment. For developments involving offshore oil and gas projects and pipelines, marine fish farming, harbour works and such terrestrial activities that may involve discharges or potential spillages to the marine environment, assessment of likely effects on marine or estuarine ecosystems will also be required.

Habitat Loss

The most obvious direct effect of development is the removal or change (e.g. through draining) of a habitat. This can be caused by the development itself, by access routes or by contractors' compounds, working or lay down areas. Typical direct losses may include individuals of species using the site, their feeding grounds, breeding areas or refuges.

Biodiversity Action Plans (BAPs)

Biodiversity Action Plans (BAPs) prioritize species and habitats for conservation action over the next 20 years. BAPs are prepared by English Nature in partnership with the other environmental regulators, local authorities and interested parties. They are prepared at national, regional, county and local levels; Habitat Action Plans (HAPs) and Species Action Plans (SAPs) are derived from BAPs. BAPs set targets which are used by local authorities and others to guide policy and strategy

Regulators and consultees

English Nature
Wildlife Trusts
RSPB
Environment Agency
Countryside Agency
Water companies
Local authority – conservation department

Biodiversity

While some direct losses may appear to be of a relatively minor nature, developments especially linear ones such as roads, railways or pipelines may sub-divide habitats or damage and remove links between them (wildlife corridors) such as hedgerows. Such effects can threaten the viability of species dependent on critical habitat areas for foraging. Small or fragmented areas may be difficult to manage in traditional ways, e.g. heathland management by burning.

Pollution

Pollution of soils, water or air by direct discharge or spillage can alter a habitat (in some cases irrevocably) which is dependent on particular conditions. Effects may be chemical change, e.g. in pH of a watercourse altered by a new discharge, or physical, e.g. blanketing of a river bed or sensitive flora/invertebrate populations by particulates.

Microclimate

Developments especially those which emit heat or light can affect the local climate on which some species depend. For example, a new reservoir in an upland region can have a warming effect on surrounding habitats or species which may only thrive in cool conditions. Built form can completely alter local microclimate.

Groundwater

Pollution or alteration in level of groundwater on which habitats are dependent can indirectly affect the habitat.

River Regimes

Changes in rates of flow or flooding associated with new hardstanding or flood prevention schemes can affect surrounding habitats.

Disturbance

New developments bringing people in close contact with previously undeveloped areas can have particular detrimental effects via disturbance, accidents (such as fire) or trampling. Of concern in connection with new residential developments is the effect of pets (especially cats), vandalism, fly-tipping, recreational pressures and increased traffic.

Indirect Effects

Habitats at some distance and apparently not affected by a development may be at risk. For example, emissions from a power station or industrial installation can affect pollution-sensitive lichens for tens or even hundreds of miles downwind.

Methodology

Baseline Studies

Consultation and desk studies are vital steps in obtaining baseline information since local societies, recorders and naturalists will often have more intimate knowledge of a locality or particular species in that locality than the statutory consultees. (It is up to the statutory consultees and the assessor to place such information in context.)

The iterative scoping process involves both consultation with statutory and non-statutory consultees and progressive compilation of the results of baseline studies. The range of the studies and any subsequent surveys is important, e.g. for wetland SSSIs, English Nature will generally require assessment within at least 2 km. The distance around a site appropriate for obtaining existing information will vary with context; in most EIAs distances of between 1 and 10 km will apply. County and national atlases, published registers and inventories should also be consulted, although they will not necessarily be currently accurate depending on date of publication and recorder effort.

It is important to remember that the sources of all information should be stated in the assessment since its quality or timing may be questioned at a later date. If there is doubt it is often worth updating such information.

Desk studies, often in association with a preliminary site visit, generally identify the necessity for field surveys. In some cases, baseline studies may have to be more extensive for lesser known sites since SSSIs or Nature Reserves may be subject to more regular survey and monitoring. Frequently, however, data relating to such sites is either unreliably historical, or inadequately precise in detail or location to permit adequate ecological assessment. In parallel with the desk study, aerial photographs are particularly useful especially for large areas or to identify changes in communities.

The simplest standard field survey is known as Phase I Habitat Survey (Nature Conservancy Council 1993). This identifies all the habitats within the area of search.

Phase I Habitat Survey includes the requirement for making lists of dominant species of plant, measuring areas of each habitat type and commenting on any features likely to be of particular local interest for wildlife or which do not fit one of the standard habitat classifications by use of target notes.

It is really designed however for large-scale habitat mapping rather than impact assessment: it makes allowance, for example, for areas to be surveyed 'remotely'. For this reason the Institute of Environmental Assessment developed the concept of an Extended Phase I Habitat Survey, which, while using exactly the same mapping symbols, entails close investigation in the field to check for the presence or absence of valued fauna. Extended Phase I Habitat Survey should, therefore, be the preliminary field survey requirement in most proposed development

Biodiversity

contexts, certainly for the proposed development footprint. Phase 1 Habitat Survey can be undertaken to provide at least an understanding of surrounding habitats and features that may be of value to mobile fauna which also utilize the site.

Protected species include fungi, lichens, bryophytes, higher plants, invertebrates, fish, amphibians, reptiles, birds and mammals listed in the Schedules of the Wildlife and Countryside Act 1981 (as amended). The protection afforded to different species varies. Some are only protected against sale, others are fully protected against any injury, or any damage to their habitat. A number of species are also protected through listing on Schedules of the Habitats Regulations. These 'European protected species' are particularly strongly protected against adverse effects resulting from development and are subject to stringent licensing procedures. Badgers and their setts are also protected under the Protection of Badgers Act 1992.

For developments including watercourses, River Corridor Surveys (RCS) or River Habitat Surveys (RHS) are often undertaken. The RCS maps habitats, vegetation and physical features of the bank and adjacent land in 500 m linear sections. Again target notes are useful since the RCS tends to focus on dominant plant species. River Habitat Surveys focus on physical features and by comparison of results with those in the national database

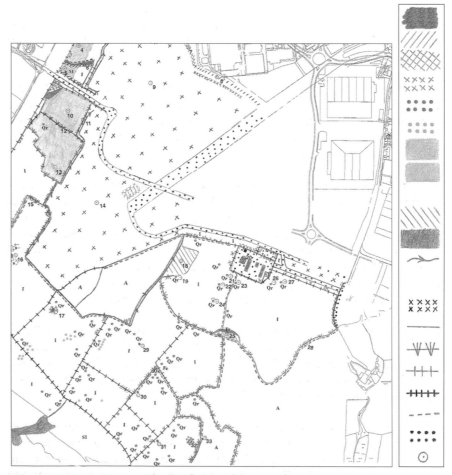

Example of map produced following Extended Phase 1 Habitat Survey with target notes (original in colour)

may be used to put the value of a watercourse in its wider context. In the most sensitive sites, e.g. river SACs, exact locational mapping (using Geographical Positioning Systems) of river habitats and features may be required. (Water quality evaluations using biological indicators or measurements are referred to in Section 3.7.)

If the desk and Extended Phase I Habitat studies identify particular valued features as being sensitive or vulnerable to development impacts, further detailed surveys will be required. At this stage the developer should be advised of the potential problem so that alternative approaches can be agreed or additional funding for survey be resourced. Such surveys may be termed Phase 2 or 3 depending on the level of detail involved and may need repeating in subsequent years. For example, there may be a need for a more detailed survey of plants to permit categorization of communities according to the National Vegetation Classification (NVC) or of particular species of conservation value or with legal protection status, e.g. bats.

Methodologies for species survey are becoming ever more detailed and standardized. If data is collected regarding protected species it is often advisable that such information is kept confidential to reduce the risk of subsequent illicit disturbance or damage. When contacting local recorders in this respect, it is important to reassure them that such information will only be made available to English Nature and will not enter the public domain without prior agreement.

Ecological resources vary in extent and detectability both within and between years. It is, therefore, important to plan surveys well in advance. For example, absence of breeding amphibians from a pond in one year does not prove that the pond is not important to amphibians.

A hedgerow survey may be required for a hedgerow in excess of 20 years old and which meets one or more of the detailed criteria as set out in the Hedgerow Regulations 1997 and associated guidance notes. Consultation with early edition Ordnance Survey maps may be required for this survey to assist in the assessment.

Marine or estuarine conditions are subject to the continuous changes brought about by coastal processes, sedimentation, water quality and tidal flows. The Environment Agency, DEFRA or the water company may be able to provide background data. It may be necessary to undertake an underwater survey using vessels for sampling and divers for observation of topography and habitats. Specific habitat guides should be used for sub-tidal habitats and the Marine Nature Conservation Review categorizes habitats in marine and estuarine environments.

Detailed criteria and outline survey evaluation methods for Phase 2 and other surveys are provided in the IEA 1995 Guidelines for Baseline Ecological Assessment. It should be noted that such guidance is being constantly updated on different types of animal, plant and habitat. Expert advice is necessary in order to follow current best practice.

It is important to record the date and time of survey. If it is not the most appropriate time of year for survey, the reasons should be stated providing all necessary caveats regarding the level of comprehensiveness and reliability of the results. Field surveyors may need to be licensed when conducting surveys for protected species.

guiding principle

Ecological surveys have to be planned well in advance due to access and seasonal constraints

guiding principle

Some surveys and assessments may require interaction between specialists, e.g. ecologists, archaeologists, and landscape architects

case example

For a proposed development adjacent to an estuarine Ramsar site, specific behavioural and population studies of wildfowl were required. These had to be repeated over several years as required by planning conditions and were subject to statistical analysis and interpretation. As a result of the wetland mitigation measures provided, wildfowl numbers actually increased with no deleterious effects on the Ramsar site.

Biodiversity

The NATA system for defining levels of effects relies on the concept of **ecological integrity**, which relates to the long-term survival of species, habitats and populations

– Highways Agency 2000

Valued Ecosystem Components (VECs)

Ecological impact assessment requires identification of selected VECs and the likelihood, nature, magnitude and duration of interaction between the VECs and changes brought about by the proposed development

Evaluation

Various values can be placed on biodiversity and there are many systems of ecological evaluation. The following criteria from IEEM (2002) are suggested:

- the conservation of genetic diversity
- direct human amenity, benefits in terms of mental and physical well-being, and value for education
- economic value.

The ecological assessment should concentrate on the first of these, but also identify the importance of biodiversity on and near a site in terms of the other criteria.

Most of the elements which contribute to the process of quantifying features or processes are covered by the Ratcliffe Criteria (Ratcliffe 1977). These include the size of populations or areas, rarity of features, species-richness and diversity, fragility of a habitat, whether a feature is a good example of its kind and how modified it is by humans. Other criteria can, and should be considered, including whether habitats can be readily recreated.

One published system for ecological valuation is that produced by the Highways Agency/English Nature the *New Approach to Appraisal* (NATA). This system reflects the different values for habitats and species under established designation systems and lists of conservation concern.

Traditionally, effects have been placed on an ordinal scale such as negligible, minor, moderate or major, and can be either positive or negative. A description of the effects of development on VECs is largely a matter of professional judgement and opinion as there are no universally accepted standardized definitions of different levels of effect. All effects should also be assigned levels of probability of occurring.

Once effects have been described the significance of these effects needs to be considered. Again, there are no universally accepted standardized definitions of significance of these effects. The implications of whether an effect of the proposed development is of such importance that it should lead to the redesign of a scheme, or require particular effort to mitigate it or compensate may depend on local community values and will be decided by the planning process. *Quality of Life Capital* (Countryside Agency, English Nature, Environment Agency, English Heritage, 2000) is one technique which may help decide such values.

Mitigation

An ecological enhancement and mitigation strategy should be based on what is trying to be achieved. For example, the locality may be the subject of a Biodiversity Action Plan (BAP). This will have been identified during consultation and may provide the framework for mitigation and enhancement measures.

A wide range of mitigation measures have been developed in recent years and experience on their value is still being gained. The principles associated with the hierarchy of avoid, reduce, remedy as recommended by the UK government should be applied.

Avoidance

- Locate development and access routes away from areas of ecological interest.
- Protect such areas from encroachment during construction and occupation.
- Avoid working during sensitive periods, e.g. the bird nesting season.
- Preserve wildlife corridors.

Reduction

- Modify design to incorporate protection measures, e.g. silt traps.
- Exclude species prior to construction.

Remedy

- Remove and replace *in situ* important features, e.g. hedgerows, grassland turves.
- Provide artificial habitats, e.g. otter holts.
- Relocate – provide appropriate receptor sites.

The effectiveness of habitat relocation is still subject to debate and, while it may have been used in previous years, success has often been limited. Accordingly, it should only be attempted as a last resort. Ancient woodlands cannot be recreated and while new planting of appropriate species can be instigated in their stead this will in no sense replace them. Moreover, local planning authorities may not accept translocation of an old and valuable habitat as adequate mitigation even if it is biologically successful because of the loss of the historical context of the original location.

It is essential to ensure that mitigation measures for one potential impact do not have negative implications for other resources, not only those of ecology.

case example

Greenwich Millennium Site

Environment Agency objectives include enhancement of the River Thames edge throughout the London tideway. The Millennium scheme contributed to this by creating and planting riverbank tidal terraces at the Greenwich Peninsula. The Greenwich Village development has also incorporated an Ecological Park for conservation and amenity interests.

Examples of Mitigation Measures at Stages of Development

Construction	Examples
Timing	Avoid nesting, breeding, flowering periods
Protection	Fencing off sensitive areas
Pollution control	Secure storage, sediment traps
Education	Briefing of site workers
Environmental Management	Implementation of Environmental Management Plan (EMP) and appointment of site environmental managers

Operation/occupation	
Preservation	Retention of valuable habitats and corridors
Design	Planting/creation of new habitat and inclusion of buffer zone around site in master plan
Pollution control	Provision of reed beds or sediment traps
Funding	Ensuring long-term provision for and implementation of management

Restoration (if applicable)	
Design	New hedgerows, habitats, ponds
Management	Long-term site monitoring and aftercare

Soils and Agriculture

Sources of Information

Type of Information

Designated areas, habitats and species
Detailed survey data and local knowledge

Sources of Information

Local Planning Authority
English Nature
Environment Agency
Local Wildlife Trust
Local Biological Records Centre
Royal Society for the Protection of Birds (RSPB)
Botanical Society for British Isles
British Trust for Ornithology
Natural History Societies
Vincent Wildlife Trust
Local recorders, specialists and natural historians

Key Features

- Early and thorough consultation and scoping, continued iteratively throughout the EIA.

- Surveys, methods of assessment and timescales vary with different species. Ecological assessment needs careful planning to ensure sufficient time in the development and authorization programme. A clear statement of timing of surveys with explanation of reasons for any sub-optimal survey timing should be included in the ES.

- Brownfield sites may be ecologically valuable compared to greenfield sites.

3.6 Soils and Agriculture, Contaminated Land and Geology

Introduction

The EIA Regulations state the need to describe and assess impacts on soils if they are likely to be significantly affected by a proposed development, and also include the need to estimate any soil pollution likely from a development. As discussed in Section 3.9, the definition of 'material assets' may be interpreted to include impacts on mineral resources and agricultural activities. The DOE Good Practice Guide (1995) defines soils as including the top and subsoil and underlying superficial deposits, and that loss of and damage to geological, palaeontological and physiographic features should also be assessed. The EIA 'Guide to

We know more about the movement of celestial bodies than about the soil underfoot

– Attributed to Leonardo da Vinci

the Procedures' (2000) states that the quality of agricultural land, solid geology, hydrogeology and minerals resources should also be taken into account.

Renewal of mineral permissions (ROMPs) require EIA for their registration and review (EIA Regulations amended 2000).

Discussion

> **The inter-related functions of soils**
>
> ■ Storage, filtration and release of rainwater influencing flood risks.
> ■ Support for all terrestrial habitats, plant and animal communities.
> ■ Providing raw materials.
> ■ Providing a platform for built development.
> ■ Protection of archaeological remains.

As soils and geology greatly influence the vegetation, hydrology, groundwater, and land use in an area, effects are linked to landscape, flora, fauna, water, air, cultural heritage and material assets. Some geological formations and soils are also of importance as mineral resources, or for earth science (e.g. coastal cliffs), archaeology and nature conservation (e.g. where caves provide habitat for bats). Ground conditions and their suitability for development are mainly determined by geological and soil conditions. Soils may also be polluted by previous industrial or urban uses and contaminants may present risks to human health or the environment.

In the past, soils have often been taken too much for granted in policy-making and planning, without specific soil protection legislation or adopted government policies. A draft Soils Strategy for the UK has now been prepared (2001) which addresses the particular concerns of the loss of soils to development and the reuse of contaminated sites.

Concern at the unnecessary loss of 'greenfield' sites to development when derelict sites are available in urban areas has led to a national target for 60% of all new dwellings to be provided on previously developed land by the year 2008, as expressed in the revised PPG 3 (2000) and the Urban White Paper (2001). PPG 3 also introduced the 'sequential' approach to housing development, which prioritizes the development of previously used sites in urban areas before the release of greenfield land. Brownfield and derelict land often has significant ecological value – greenfield land by contrast, may have low ecological value.

Contaminated land is now defined by the Contaminated Land Regulations with regard to significant harm (to human health, buildings, livestock, water, flora and fauna) or pollution. The nature and extent of the contamination and proposals for remediation should be included in EIA; contaminated land investigation and remediation can be expensive and time-consuming. Developers are often reticent to include details of surveys and remediation strategies for reasons of:

Key fact

Soils should be accorded the same priority in environmental protection policies as air and water

– RCEP 1996

Key fact

Government guidance favours the reuse of brownfield land, such sites may not be suitable for sustainable development given contamination, access and biodiversity issues

Key legislation & guidance

Environmental Protection Act 1990
Environment Act 1995
Contaminated Land Regulations 2000
PPG 3 Housing 2000
PPG 7 The Countryside 1997
PPG 14 Development on Unstable Land 1990
PPG 23 Planning and Pollution Control 1994 (under revision)
Minerals Planning Guidance 7
The Reclamation of Mineral Workings Rural White Paper 2000
Urban White Paper 2000
UK draft Soils Strategy 2001
Circular 02/00 Contaminated land

Key fact

The Environment Agency estimates that up to 300,000 hectares of land are affected by industrial or natural contamination

Soils and Agriculture

Key fact

PPG 23 is under revision and a key issue is that the responsibility for providing information of whether land is contaminated rests primarily with the developer

case example

An ES for a major pipeline classified all soil types along the pipeline route through desk study and soil survey, and went on to identify significant potential impacts and mitigation measures for farm structure, soil excavation, handling, storage and reinstatement.

Regulators and consultees

Soils and agriculture

DEFRA; Farming and Rural Conservation Agency; farmers; National Farmers Union; landowners; Country Landowners Association

Contaminated land

Environment Agency, Local Authorities (District Councils)

Geology

Minerals Planning Authority (County Councils); Coal Authority; British Geological Society; English Nature; local RIGS Group

case example

Outline redevelopment proposals for housing on a former munitions factory in Enfield, north London were initially accompanied by an ES, which proposed a comprehensive Reclamation Strategy based on an initial field survey of ground contamination. Areas of greatest contamination, as identified by further detailed site investigations, were to be removed off site and all contaminated materials to be removed from residential areas. Subsequently new developers submitted revised remediation strategies for site development, which were eventually approved in 1997 amid local controversy. Local groups and the Environment Agency, given a special 'extended' remit by the government to offer good practice advice to the Council, warned that the site surveys and precautions proposed for the 'capping' of contaminated soils in areas proposed for housing were inadequate. A subsequent report by London Friends of the Earth and Enfield Lock Action Group, and a Panorama TV programme, questioned the ability of the planning system to ensure the adequate remediation of risks to health and the environment from contaminated land which is being redeveloped when local councils can ignore specialist advice from the Environment Agency.

- confidentiality
- commitment to costs
- public perception and acceptability.

However, an ES with limited information may risk the success of the planning application; the ES must include sufficient information to enable assessment of impacts.

Soils tend to be an important topic for EIA where:

- soils need to be disturbed to enable a development (e.g. a pipeline or minerals workings), and later reinstated for continued use for agriculture, forestry, recreation, or conservation
- high quality agricultural land may be disturbed or lost to development
- existing land contamination is suspected or known.

Reviews of ESs have revealed that soils and geology appear to be considered among the least important issues in EIA. However, as indicated above, an understanding of the soils and geology of a site and the surrounding area is necessary for a range of other EIA topics recognizing their interactions.

Regulators and Consultees

Soils and Agriculture

DEFRA (and its Farming and Rural Conservation Agency) are consulted on development proposals affecting agricultural land. Farmers and landowners (including their representatives where appropriate, e.g. National Farmers Union and Country Landowners Association) should also be consulted.

Agri-environment schemes aim to promote agricultural practices that conserve the landscape, wildlife and heritage features, both in DEFRA designated Environmentally Sensitive Areas and in the wider countryside through the Countryside Stewardship Scheme.

Contaminated Land

The Contaminated Land Regulations 2000 require local authorities to inspect their areas and identify contaminated land which requires remediation. The Environment Agency is responsible for the most contaminated 'special sites', and is also a statutory consultee where development is within 250 m of a waste landfill site. Local Authorities and the Environment Agency should therefore be consulted where land contamination is suspected.

The instability of land may be a material consideration for site development and Local Authorities and mining organizations should be consulted where instability, e.g. on slopes or from previous mining activities, is suspected. Minerals Planning Authorities (County Councils) should also be consulted in areas where planning policies protect minerals resources from sterilization by development. Geological features and biological sites (of which soil is an inherent part) of national importance are protected as SSSIs and designated by English Nature. Non-statutory Regionally Important Geological and Geomorphological Sites (RIGS) are identified by the county RIGS Group.

Potential Effects

Most developments will affect soils and their functions in some way through loss (by removal, or increased erosion of base soils by rain and wind), or through physical and chemical damage of soils (largely compaction, disaggregation, contamination), including those which are removed and stored for reinstatement. Compaction of soils by heavy vehicles and storage of materials is common and this can reduce water and root penetration leading to waterlogging, increased run-off and erosion, and reduced plant growth. The nature of the soils present will determine the likely severity of the impacts, as different soil types are more or less susceptible to different impacts depending on their composition.

The potential secondary effects arising from impacts on the soil on water, land use, landscape, nature conservation and cultural heritage, and the implications for the development proposals, should also be considered. Agricultural land taken by development can affect the viability of continued farming activities over a wider area, and temporary disruption to farm access can be created by pipelines, transport routes and temporary roads. Increased public access to an area due to development may also lead to effects on a farm holding, e.g. through recreational activities, vandalism, fly-tipping, as well as positive effects of potential increased viability through farm diversification. The development of agricultural land may also affect features protected by landscape, wildlife or heritage designations, or have implications for the conservation of areas promoted by agri-environment schemes. Soil movement along pipeline spreads or other linear developments can also risk the spread of disease.

Development of land which is contaminated but not currently causing harm or pollution can lead to significant risks through public exposure or mobilization of contaminants. As some of the liability associated with contaminated land may be passed on through land purchase, buyers of potentially contaminated land will need to carry out pre-purchase audits of such land to be fully aware of any such liabilities. Development near landfill sites can also be susceptible to the migration of landfill gas and leachate.

Geological issues can include the instability of slopes, the presence of geological faults, underground mine working and impacts on groundwater movement, underground cavities and potential for ground collapse, effects on coastal processes, the presence and potential sterilization of mineral resources, and impacts on earth science conservation. In particular, development affecting coastal cliffs and erosion can have significant effects away from the site itself.

Methodology

Investigations are usually required to determine the ground conditions and underlying geology of a site to determine the stability of the land

Key fact

All applications for development on 'greenfield' sites of over 150 houses or housing on over 5 ha must be notified to the Secretary of State

"

Contaminated land '*is land which appears to the local authority ... to be in such a condition, by reason of substances in, or on or under the land, that **significant harm** is being caused or there is a significant possibility of such harm being caused; or pollution of controlled waters is being or is likely to be caused.' The Regulations further define 'significant harm'*

– Contaminated Land Regulations   "

guiding principle

Assessment of contaminated land is based on the '*suitable for use*' approach which considers risks to human health and the environment

Soils and Agriculture

and the specific engineering requirements for building foundations, pipelines, minerals workings and waste disposal sites.

Early consideration of the likely significance of potential effects and the importance of soils, geology and agricultural land uses is needed to determine the scope and level of baseline studies and impact assessments that are required.

Baseline conditions

If only a brief description of soil types is required for an EIA, a desk study may be adequate to determine the general properties of soils. The Soil Survey and Land Research Centre holds the national soil maps and accompanying booklets which describe the soil classifications and related geology and land uses.

Land is classified into Agricultural Land Classification (ALC) grades 1–5 with grades 1, 2 and 3a forming the best and most versatile land.

Key fact

ALC Maps do not differentiate between land classification 3a and 3b and consequently site surveys are often required

Maps of land quality for agricultural uses are available from the Farming and Rural Conservation Agency (FRCA) (although these do not differentiate between ALC grades 3a and 3b). The results of more detailed ALC surveys carried out for local authorities, and information on farm holdings and agricultural land uses on a parish basis, may also be available from the FRCA.

Where a development potentially involves the loss or disturbance of the 'best and most versatile' agricultural land, site surveys by specialist soil scientists may be needed to confirm mapped information or determine the precise ALC grades affected. Soil surveys may also be needed to determine the soil classification and properties in more detail than is available from maps. Field surveys usually involve a combination of hand auger boring and (more informative) soil pits over the site in a systematic grid pattern or focussing on specific areas of interest. Soils surveys consider physical characteristics and chemical analysis.

If agricultural activities are to be significantly affected by a development, discussions and consultation should be held with affected farmers and landowners, to ascertain the land uses and activities affected.

An initial desk study of a site's history should reveal whether contamination by previous uses is suspected or considered likely; this comprises a review of all available historic maps, site records from previous occupiers, local archives and histories. The public registers that local authorities are required to keep will identify all the known contaminated land in their areas once inspections have been undertaken. The National Land Use Database developed by the Department of Environment, Transport and the Regions/Department of Transport, Local Government and the Regions (DETR/DTLR) and others will attempt to provide information on previously used and derelict or under-used sites considered suitable for residential development to local authorities to facilitate their redevelopment. The Environment Agency keeps records of former waste disposal sites. The series of Industry Profiles produced by the DOE provides initial information to help identify and assess risks and remedial measures for a

guiding principle

Early discussion with the Environment Agency and the Local authority to agree to the appropriate level of site investigations (SIs) can avoid later conflict and delays wide range of contaminative uses such as gas works and types of chemical works.

Site surveys will be required in areas to be developed that are suspected to be contaminated to determine the nature and extent of contamination that may present risks to human health, water pollution, animals and plants. A systematic grid pattern of trial pits and boreholes at specified locations and depths are generally required. Analysis undertaken will vary according to type of contamination and the options for end-use.

The geology of an area can usually be determined through reference to the British Geological Survey (BGS) maps of solid and drift geology, and to mining and quarrying records held by the Coal Authority and others, although reliable records may only relate to the late 19th century onwards. Local authorities should also have access to good information on any land instability problems in their areas. Information on workable minerals resources will be held by the Minerals Planning Authority; the Environment Agency (EA) will hold maps showing the vulnerability of groundwater, and maps of geological SSSIs are available from English Nature. Local biological or environmental record centres usually have further information on RIGS sites.

Intrusive geotechnical surveys including boreholes at specified locations will be required as appropriate to the proposed development and likely site conditions. Surveys should aim to determine both conditions likely to be affected and those likely to affect the development and future users of a site.

To determine the significance of contamination, the level of potential contaminants detected are commonly compared with the 'threshold' and 'action' levels established for a limited range of substances listed in the non-statutory ICRCL 1987 guidelines. This guidance is under revision and will be superseded by the forthcoming DEFRA publications on risk assessment and management of contaminated land under the new regulatory regime. Until UK guidance is revised, many developers have found it useful to use the more recent and comprehensive 'Dutch A–B–C values'. Guidance on the investigation of potentially contaminated sites is now available in BS 10175: 2001.

Project Description

General considerations apply to many types of development and include: the area and nature of permanent and temporary land take, the nature and location of permanent structures, the depth and nature of excavations, the nature of excavated materials, re-use of materials on site or disposal off-site, working methods for soil removal and storage, any requirements for re-use of soils, site restoration and after-use, the timescale and phasing of development and season of working, potential for on-site or off-site soil treatment, materials used in contact with soils, access requirements for vehicles including temporary roads, requirements for storage of fuels and materials.

Impact Prediction and Significance

The significance of direct losses of soil are usually dependent on the extent of the loss or disruption and grade of land affected. Temporary

Soils and Agriculture

disturbance of soils, e.g. for pipelines, mineral and waste developments, has been regarded as significant where the quality of the restored soil has deteriorated by an ALC grade. The net loss of soils to development is now identified as a headline indicator in the UK Sustainable Development Strategy. The significance of effects on soil should also be assessed with reference to secondary effects on groundwater infiltration, flood risks, cultural heritage, flora and fauna, and the landscape character. Effects from a development on the viability of farm holdings from land take or severance can be assessed using financial formulae.

Current government guidance is that the redevelopment of contaminated land should be remediated to reduce risks to an acceptable level suitable for its current and intended use. Non-statutory UK ICRCL Guidelines and Dutch values for lists of chemical contaminants, together with water quality standards for contaminants polluting the water environment, are used to assess significance and guide remediation strategies. The significance of the residual risks and impacts potentially arising from the redevelopment of contaminated land and best practice guidance for risk assessment under the Contaminated Land Regulations 2000 is awaited from government.

Assessing the effects of a development on geological features and processes requires a knowledge of similar cases and the application of sound scientific principles. Assessments of ground conditions and land instability need to take account of conditions outside the site boundary and of potential variations in climate, as excessive rainfall or periods of drought can change ground and groundwater conditions.

Mitigation

Good practice techniques for the stripping, handling, storage and reinstatement of soils can reduce the inevitable loss of and damage to soils (from erosion, compaction, disaggregation and pollution) from development. This ensures that soils can be adequately reinstated for their previous uses or re-used as a growing medium within a development site. General requirements include limiting wet weather working, minimizing exposure of soils (especially on slopes), restricting heavy traffic movements to dedicated haul roads, fencing off land not required for development, avoid mixing of different soil materials, decompaction of soil after reinstatement (although this affects the soil structure), and prevention of pollution through adequate storage of fuels and other materials.

Mitigation for temporary disruption of agricultural activities can involve changes to the routes or timing of works, maintaining access to fields for farm machinery or livestock, and ensuring adequate protection and reinstatement of the soil, field drainage and boundaries, and taking account of any requirements of agri-environment schemes such as no fertiliser use. Adverse effects from increased public access may be reduced to some extent by waymarking, fencing or diversion of footpaths.

A contaminated site has been 'remediated' where the land is suitable for use and previous contamination does not cause any significant harm or pollution. To demonstrate a site is remediated it must be ensured that each potential pollutant linkage is no longer significant by:

Key fact

The Contaminated Land Regulations use the concept of a **pollutant linkage**, i.e. a linkage between a **contaminant** and a **receptor**, by means of a **pathway**. Contamination cannot cause pollution unless there is a pathway to the receptor. The Regulations give guidance on the types of receptor; the degree or nature of significant harm; and the degree of possibility of significant harm being caused.

- removing the pollutant
- treating the pollutant
- breaking or removing the pathway that causes harm
- protecting or removing the receptor; or
- remedying the effect of any significant harm or pollution.

Treatment or containment options that avoid removing the contamination elsewhere (usually to landfill) are generally preferable, although a Waste Management Licence may be required for treatment, and the advice of the Environment Agency should be sought. DEFRA is producing a framework of model procedures for the selection of remedial measures in the redevelopment of contaminated land. Publications by DEFRA, DETR, Environment Agency and CIRIA also describe best practice techniques for a range of *'in situ'* and off-site treatment options. Biological treatment methods are appropriate for certain contaminants and are potentially more sustainable. However, the landtake and time for, e.g. composting needs to be integrated into the development schedule.

Careful design of a development is the best way of mitigating any significant impacts on geological features or processes, and avoiding significant risks to the development.

Sources of Information

Department for Environment, Food and Rural Affairs (DEFRA)
Environment Agency
Farming and Rural Conservation Agency
Soil Survey and Land Research Centre, Cranfield University, Silsoe
British Geological Survey
Construction Industry Research and Information Association (CIRIA)

Further information

RCEP 1996. 19th Report – The Sustainable Use of Soil

Town and Country Planning (Residential Development on Greenfield Land) (England) Direction 2000

MAFF 1993. Code of Good Agricultural Practice for the Protection of Soil

MAFF 2000. Good practice guide for handling soils

DOE 1987. Interdepartmental Committee on the Redevelopment of Contaminated Land (ICRCL) Guidance Note 59/83

DOE 1996. Guidance on Good Practice for the reclamation of mineral working to agriculture

Environment Agency/National House Building Council 2000. Guidance for the Safe Development of Housing on Land Affected by Contamination

BSI 1999. BS5930: Code of practice for site investigations

BSI 1990. BS1377: Methods of test for soils for engineering purposes

BSI many parts with various dates, BS7755, Soil quality

BSI 2001. BS10175 Investigation of potentially contaminated sites: Code of practice

BSI 1989. BS8010-1 Code of practice for pipelines: pipelines on land

Key Features

- Soils have largely been taken for granted in the past in environmental planning and the government is producing a soils strategy to attempt to increase the priority given to soil protection as a key part of sustainable development.

- Soils and geology may not always be major topics in their own right in an EIA. However, it is usually necessary in EIA to investigate the geology and types of soil on and around a site to be able to determine not only the potential effects on the soil and geological resources in their own right, but also to fully understand the interactions with other environmental issues.

- Government policies increasingly aim to minimize loss of soils and agricultural land to development and promote the safe redevelopment of contaminated land. A new regime for investigation and assessment of risks from contaminated land is being introduced by DEFRA.

3.7 Water

Introduction

If the water environment is likely to be significantly affected by the proposed development then the EIA Regulations require a description of the existing conditions or state, the likely significant effects and measures envisaged to prevent, reduce or offset such adverse effects on water.

The water environment includes consideration of environmental protection (both related to public health and the natural environment), and the use of natural resources.

Key legislation and guidance

Environment Act 1995

Water Resources Act 1991

Water Industry Act 1991

Land Drainage Act 1991

PPC Regulations 2000

Control of Pollution Regulations 1996

Groundwater Regulations 1998

Contaminated Land Regulations 2000

EU Water Framework Directive 2000

PPG 20 Coastal Planning

PPG 23 Planning and Pollution Control 1994

PPG 25 Development and Flood Risk 2001

Policy and Practice for the Protection of Floodplains, Environment Agency

Policy and Practice for the Protection of Groundwater, Environment Agency, 1998

Aspects of the Water Environment and Development

- Surface water
    Watercourses (rivers and canals)
    Reservoirs, lakes and ponds
    Wetlands
- Groundwater
- Estuarine and coastal waters
- Flood risk management
    Flood defence (fluvial and coastal)
- Land drainage
- Infrastructure
    Wastewater treatment and sewerage
    Water supply
- Recreation and amenity
- Biodiversity
- Navigation and transport

There is specific legislation and guidance relating to pollution control, water abstraction, flood management, land drainage, nature conservation and navigation, and this needs to be addressed in parallel with the EIA process.

European legislation relating to water has been largely unified under the Water Framework Directive (2000/60/EC). UK Regulations to implement the directive are due in 2003 (see below).

The selection criteria for screening Schedule 2 development draws special attention to the use of natural resources, the production of waste and pollution and the environmental sensitivity of the geographical areas likely to be affected by development, having regard to the absorption capacity of the natural environment including wetlands and those areas in which environmental quality standards laid down in Community legislation have already been exceeded.

Discussion

Some significant water related projects are subject to EIA under non-planning regulations. In particular, land drainage improvement works such as the repair or renewal of river control structures require EIA if the works are likely to have significant effects on the environment.

Works below the low water mark, e.g. for new ports or harbours, marine fish farming, marine dredging or works under the Transport and Works Act 1992 (which can include interference with navigation or new waterways) all may require EIA and application to the appropriate authority (e.g. DEFRA, DTLR, Crown Estates).

Flooding is a natural process and floodplains, by definition, act to contain the additional water from rivers in flood conditions. Development in floodplains will therefore be generally resisted by the Environment Agency and developers will be required to provide for flood compensation elsewhere, fund flood defences or provide flood warning measures.

Redevelopment in the floodplain will be required to use Sustainable Urban Drainage Systems (SUDS) so as not to increase surface water runoff. Maintenance and adoption are the key issues for implementation of SUDS and commitment should be made in the ES to this form of mitigation. Consideration of the application of SUDS should be at project inception stage and include ecological and landscape designers within the project team.

> The complexity of monitoring, regulating, using and protecting the water environment has led to a plethora of **water-related planning regimes**:
>
> Catchment Abstraction Management Strategies (CAMS)
> Coastal Habitat Management Plans (CHaMPS)
> Coastal Zone Management (CZM)
> Estuary Management Plans (EMPs)
> Flood Management Plans
> Local Environment Agency Plans (LEAPs)
> River Basin Management Plans (RBMPs) by 2009
> Shoreline Management Plans (SMPs)
> Water Level Management Plans (WLMPs)
> Water Resource Strategies.

Key fact

The Environment Agency produces s105 maps (WRA91) to show flood risk areas

guiding principle

New development should use SUDS wherever practicable

Key fact

PPG 25 requires joint strategies with planners, drainage boards or authorities, sewerage undertakers and the Environment Agency to encourage the use of SUDS

Water

> **The EU Water Framework Directive 2000**
>
> The implementation of this directive into UK regulations will integrate the existing diverse directives on the water environment including: bathing waters, dangerous substances, drinking water quality, ecological quality, freshwater fish and shellfish waters, groundwater protection, nitrate pollution from agriculture, surface water abstraction, surface water quality and urban waste water treatment.
>
> The framework requires River Basin Districts (RBDs) to be identified as the main unit for managing the water environment. Analysis will include the characteristics of each RBD, review the environmental impact of human activities, and the economic use of water.

The issues relating to water management and proposed development are exacerbated by the predicted effects of climate change, which include:

- increased risk of flooding
- reduced groundwater recharge
- increased demand for public water supply and irrigation.

This is further discussed in Section 3.8.

Proposed development can offer the possibility of restoration of a watercourse; an enhanced water environment can facilitate regeneration.

The amenity aspects of urban drainage, such as community facilities, landscaping potential and provision of varied wildlife habitats have largely been ignored

– CIRIA 2000

We will work with all sections of the community to reduce flood risks through preventive planning, restoration of rivers and floodplains, better management of the disposal of surface water and better design of buildings

– An Environmental Vision Environment Agency 2000

Key fact

The Environment Agency will always insist on access provision alongside main rivers of at least 8 m

Regulators and Consultees

Environment Agency

- grants licences to abstract or impound water under WRA91
- sets discharge consents under WRA91
- sets Water Quality Objectives for rivers
- provides guidance and advice on pollution prevention and control
- issues permits and regulates prescribed activities under PPC regulations (emissions to air, land and water)
- controls groundwater resources through Groundwater Regulations and WRA91 – groundwater vulnerability maps, Source Protection Zones and Nitrate Vulnerable Zones
- controls development within 8 m of main rivers (or 15 m on a tidal river) under WRA91 or construction of a structure that would affect the flow of an ordinary watercourse (Land Drainage Act 1991)
- supervision of all matters relating to flood defence and flood warning

Water Companies – plc

- provide wholesome water supply under WIA91
- provide and maintain the sewerage system for the transfer of sewage to treatment works
- set and provide trade effluent standards and consents for discharges to sewers under WIA91.

Water Companies – private

- provide water supplies only.

Local Authorities

- regulate private water supplies
- regulate bathing waters (monitored on their behalf by the Environment Agency)
- undertake flood defence work on non-main rivers (outside Internal Drainage Board – IDB – districts)
- powers to protect land against coastal erosion, encroachment or flooding by the sea (maritime authorities).

Department of Environment, Food and Rural Affairs

- responsible for flood and coastal defence policy
- responsible for control of fisheries.

Others

British Waterways
Port and Harbour Authorities
Port Health Authorities
Sea Fisheries Committees
IDBs
English Nature
Wetland and Wildfowl Trust
RSPB
Angling, recreation, watersport , conservation and boat user groups.

Potential Effects

The potential effects on the water environment can conveniently be divided into those of physical effects, quantity (hydrological/hydrogeological) and quality (pollution).

Physical Effects

These include:

- canalization of a river to increase channel capacity and rapid removal of floodwaters
- removal of ponds or lakes
- diversion of a watercourse
- construction of a dam, creating a new upstream reservoir and alterations to downstream flow regimes – with consequences for siltation in both the watercourse and the reservoir
- dredging to increase depth of water
- construction of weirs as barrages preventing tidal effects, salinity and exposure or passage of migrating fish
- coastal defences affecting natural coastal processes of erosion and siltation/deposition.

> **guiding principle**
>
> Effects on the water environment are rarely in isolation: amenity and ecology are also affected. The indirect effects must be remembered

Water

Quantity

Development can change the nature of the land and its ability to absorb or manage rainfall. Frequently, extensive paved areas and storm water drainage are included within development which reduces the time taken for water to reach watercourses. Peak flows are increased and recharge of groundwater is reduced as a consequence. This in turn increases the risk and frequency of flooding downstream, causes erosion on site and down-stream and reduces aquifer levels. This is particularly of importance for proposed development in floodplains.

Conversely, increased abstraction or changes to abstraction patterns from rivers or aquifers can lead to siltation and reduced flows from springs.

Developments in floodplains will require additional flood defence struc-tures and changes to the profile, form or gradient of a river. This increases the risk of flooding upstream and downstream; dredging or straightening of the river reduces habitat diversity and refuges for fish.

Reduction in aquifer levels can affect habitats dependent on water table levels. Similarly, pipelines can act as drains diverting water from its nat-ural catchment. New development places additional demands on water resource requirements further depleting aquifer levels leading to poten-tial drought conditions and supply restrictions. In certain geological conditions rivers can dry up in summer.

---

case example

Proposed Oil Pipeline

This proposed oil pipeline potentially crossed sensitive areas of the Norfolk Broads. Hydrogeological studies and ground surveys were required to select the appropriate route and technique to ensure that the pipeline would not affect these wetlands of international importance.

Quality

Water quality is dependent on geology, topography and land use as well as discharges to the aquatic environment. Pollution occurs when the receiving environment can no longer absorb the concentration of pollu-tants discharged.

For any stretch of main river the Environment Agency sets Water Quality Objectives which are based on the uses to which the river is put. Increased discharges could result in those objectives no longer being met, with a consequent effect on the users, e.g. potable abstraction by water compa-nies, recreation groups, or on habitats and fisheries. In extreme cases human health may be threatened. Pollutants include heavy metals, organic and inorganic wastes, suspended solids, toxic substances, oils and fuels, and heat.

Pollutants can enter the water environment by direct point source dis-charge from, e.g. sewage treatment works, industry or agriculture. Land uses can increase run-off from diffuse sources, e.g. roads, agriculture. Leaching of pollutants from landfills or previously contaminated land can cause pollution of groundwater or watercourses.

The addition of an excess of nutrients generally from sewage treatment or agriculture (in the form of fertilisers) can lead to eutrophication and algal blooms in surface waters. The excessive growth and life cycle of algae results in deoxygenation causing fish kills and difficulties in water treatment processes. The presence of oil films on water surfaces can

---

case example

Leeds Waterfront

The River Aire in Leeds had a legacy of industrial pollution. A partnership including Yorkshire Water, the Environment Agency and the local authorities restored the water quality of the river. This encouraged investors to redevelop the industrial warehouses fronting the river, encouraging regeneration, and the waterfront is now a vibrant area in the city. The catalyst for the regeneration was the improvement to the water quality in the river.

Photo by Hugh Howes

prevent the transfer of oxygen into the water resulting in a similar deoxygenation as well as the coating of water birds and creating aesthetic problems.

Vandalism or accidental and uncontained spillages, especially by chemicals or fuels and oils, are frequent but short-lived examples of pollution. However, once groundwater is polluted it is difficult to remedy and can result in loss of an aquifer for potable supply.

Methodology

Baseline studies

The scope of such studies is very much defined by the location of development in terms of catchment boundaries, proximity to the coast, and soil and groundwater characteristics. Considerable initial assistance and guidance can be obtained from the Environment Agency in respect of the range and extent of studies. Basic information about existing conditions, and Agency aspirations, objectives and concerns can be gathered from Local Environment Agency Plans (LEAPs). These identify, amongst other elements of the environment, discharges and abstractions, designations, habitats, water quality and objectives, aquifers and drainage patterns. Further detailed environmental data from routine monitoring programmes is available on request from the Agency or from the public register.

Scoping of the issues by consultation with the Environment Agency, water companies and others (see above) will identify the need for additional surveys as part of the baseline study. These surveys might include:

- river flow measurement
- groundwater (water table) measurement
- chemical and biological river surveys
- river corridor surveys
- river habitat surveys
- fisheries surveys
- user surveys.

Flow measurement in rivers can include the employment of special equipment and the installation of temporary weirs. Groundwater measurement may involve boreholes, trial pits or piezometers for water levels. Any surveys have to be designed over an appropriate length of time to collect meaningful data.

Chemical river surveys initiated for the purpose of undertaking a project EIA, have limited value: they are only spot checks unless integrated with a continuing programme of monitoring. Biological or fisheries surveys are of considerably more value since they will give a more accurate representation of the long-term health of the water environment. Responses to intermittent pollution may not be evident from a chemical survey. Biological surveys can also identify potential cumulative effects of discharge and synergistic effects of various pollutants.

Water pollution measurement

Physical: temperature, suspended solids, odour

Chemical: salinity, metals, pesticides

Microbiological: coliforms, viruses

Biological: fish, invertebrates, aquatic plants

Water

guiding principle

Consider all users of the water environment and potentially conflicting demands

There are potentially conflicting requirements of water users, such as those of canoeists and anglers. The needs of different users are identified in the LEAPs but more detailed user surveys may be required in some circumstances.

Project Description

All potential emissions to, or abstractions from, the water environment during both construction and operation of the proposed development should be described. This can include storage of fuels, water usage, and runoff from site activity and traffic during construction. The incorporation of water saving or recycling measures and the utilization of SUDS into the design should be reported.

Impact Prediction and Significance

Comparing the baseline conditions and trends with the activities and emissions of the proposed development will highlight those particular issues which are likely to be significant and require careful evaluation. Clearly the significance of any predicted changes will be as measured against existing standards and objectives. If consent to discharge is (or will be) granted by the Environment Agency the impact should be regarded by other regulators as acceptable. Any evaluation will need to take into account predicted changes due to global warming, i.e. sea level rise and increased severity and frequency of flooding. In order to determine the acceptability of a proposed discharge or alteration to an existing consent, the Agency uses a formula based on the strength and value of the proposed or altered discharge and the assimilative capacity of the receiving watercourse.

In order to quantify these effects of proposed discharges, modelling of coastal or fluvial processes to understand the sensitivity of the receiving environment to changes in quality or flows may be necessary. Biological predictions are possible using RIVPACS (River Invertebrate Prediction and Classification System) and scoring systems to estimate the significance of change. Predictions of groundwater effects or movement can be made based on an understanding of the underlying geology. Once the predictions have been calculated they can then be judged against the various relevant prevailing policies, guidance and standards.

If discharges are not possible or permitted to a watercourse or other waters, then discharge to the sewerage system may be an alternative to on site treatment. Such a discharge will require the system to have capacity and the consent of the water company in accordance with the Water Industry Act 1991. Charges will be levied and pre-treatment may still be required.

Mitigation

There is likely to be a range of negative impacts for an issue such as water and a mitigation strategy should be developed. The available mitigation options are naturally numerous and wide ranging depending on the nature of the impact but some are suggested opposite:

Mitigation option	Typical objective
Restoration of original channel pattern	Increases assimilative capacity of watercourse
Introduction of new channel features, e.g. oxbows	Provides enhancement to habitat and aesthetic quality
Incorporation of sustainable drainage systems	Reduces flooding by alleviating rapid changes in flow regimes and watercourses within catchment; protects water quality; provides wildlife habitat
Reduce or eliminate particular chemical from process or waste discharge	Protects environment, reduces need for treatment or transfer of flow to treatment works
Containment of storage areas/ vessels within bunded areas	Reduces risk of spillage during construction/operation
Use of sediment traps or interceptors and vegetated areas	Prevents blanketing of river bed during in-stream work and reduces levels of pollutants in run-off
Separation of clean and contaminated water	Reduces volume to be treated
Reuse of heated water	Reduces elevated temperature in receiving waters and rates of growth of algae, etc.
Creation of flood storage areas	Maintains the capacity of the floodplain to regulate river flows

---

Sustainable Urban Drainage Systems (SUDS)

SUDS are methods of managing surface water drainage to balance the impacts (quantity: quality: amenity) of urban drainage on the environment. They aim to deal with runoff close to where the rain falls to prevent flooding and reduce pollution. There are four general methods of control:

- filter strips and swales
- filter drains and permeable surfaces
- infiltration devices
- basins and ponds.

The variety of design options available allows designers and planners to consider local landuse, land take, future management and the needs of the local community.

From: SUDS Design Manual for England and Wales, DETR/CIRIA , 2000

---

case example

Two Rivers Retail Park, Staines

The redevelopment of a former trading estate for a retail development in conjunction with an Environment Agency flood protection scheme enabled the channelised watercourse to be restored and enhanced. The river now forms an attractive setting for the new development. By working in tandem, costs and responsibilities were shared between the Agency and the developer.

Photo by Hugh Howes.

Further information

www.environment-agency.gov.uk

www.defra.gov.uk

Sustainable Urban Drainage Systems, design manual for England and Wales, DETR/CIRIA 2000

A Guide to Water Quality, DETR 2000

Pollution Handbook, NSCA 2000

The River Restoration Centre
rr@cranfield.ac.uk

The Rivers and Wildlife Handbook RSPB, NRA, Wildlife Trusts, 1994

www.rspb.org.uk

CIRIA – Sustainable Construction

Sources of Information

Type	Source
Capacity of Infrastructure	Water Companies
River Water Quality	Environment Agency
Estuary Surveys	
Groundwater	
Bathing water quality	
River Flows	
Flood Risk Maps	
Discharge and abstraction	
Consents and licences	
Private Water Supplies	Local Authority Environmental Health

Key Features

- There is a plethora of regulations, plans, policies and associated regulators for the water environment, reflecting its complexity and interactions with other environmental elements.
- Development should avoid floodplains, wherever practicable.
- SUDS should be considered early and incorporated in the design of new or re-development, and arrangements identified for maintenance in the ES.
- Restoration of degraded, canalized or culverted watercourses can offer opportunities for environmental enhancement and regeneration.

> 'It isn't pollution that's harming the environment. It's the impurities in our air and water that are doing it.
>
> – George W. Bush

3.8   Air, Climate, Odour

Introduction

The EIA Regulations require air and climatic factors to be examined if they are likely to be significantly affected by a development. If significant effects are anticipated, the existing conditions need to be described together with the associated effects. In the case of air quality and climatic effects, this includes those resulting from the emission of pollutants, the creation of nuisances and the elimination of waste. Odour is not specifically referred to in the Regulations but is listed in the DETR Guide to the Procedures as a consideration within the discussion of air and climatic factors.

The UK Air Quality Strategy considers improving and maintaining air quality as a joint responsibility; with industry, the transport sector, local authorities and individuals all asked to contribute. Under Local Air Quality Management (LAQM) local authorities are required to carry out a review and assessment of air quality in their area to identify whether the objectives will be achieved by a given date. If the objectives are not expected to be met then the authority is required to declare an air quality management area and prepare an action plan setting out how it intends to work towards meeting them.

Pollution from industrial sources is controlled through the IPPC and Local Air Pollution Prevention and Control (LAPPC) regimes. IPPC requires operators to obtain a permit from the regulator (either the Environment Agency or local authority), before releasing emissions into the air, water or land. If a proposed IPPC installation requires planning permission, it is recommended that the operator should make both applications in parallel. The IPPC regulator can then start its formal consideration early on and have a more informed input to the planning process. The regulator must also take account of any information related to the EIA Directive.

Discussion

One of the key issues associated with air quality and climatic effects within EIA relates to the consideration of global effects versus local effects. Air quality assessments generally concentrate on local effects, with little or no consideration of international or global effects. The EIA Regulations do, however, require transboundary effects to be considered.

Global climate change resulting from the release of greenhouse gases is generally not considered in EIAs. Issues such as energy efficiency and CO_2 emissions are often examined in energy projects, but are rarely dealt with for infrastructure developments, such as new housing or roads. If the UK is to meet its commitments under the Kyoto Protocol then contributions from all forms of development will need to be examined and measures put in place to reduce emissions of greenhouse gases. A whole range of initiatives have been, or are being, put into place in order to reduce emissions of greenhouse gases, including the climate change levy, the Carbon Trust, the Emissions Trading Group. Additional energy efficiency requirements are also being introduced into the Building Regulations, including measures to raise performance standards for insulation and heating systems and standards of lighting. Such sustainability issues are now enshrined in the planning system: EIA can increasingly play a part in recommending measures to address them. A major implication of predicted climate change is increased risk of flooding.

At the local level, developments can affect the microclimate; cause local warming due to high levels of thermal output and changes to land cover; cause cooling due to overshadowing; and affect local winds, creating wind canyons, eddies and downdraughts.

Regulators and Consultees

Initial consultation should be with the relevant local authority Environmental Health Department. EHOs should be able to provide advice about what survey data is available and what are key concerns or issues within the local area. EHOs can also advise on the approach to the assessment of air quality – which pollutants to examine, monitoring locations and potentially sensitive receptors. It is advisable to agree the scope and approach to the assessment from the outset in order to avoid unexpected problems at a later date. (The Environment Agency and local authority are also regulators and consultees for developments subject to authorization under IPPC.)

Key legislation & guidance

Air Quality (England) Regulations 2000

Pollution Prevention and Control Regulations 2000

PPG 13 Transport

PPG 23 Planning and Pollution Control

PPG 25 Development and Flood Risk

DETR 2000. Integrated Pollution Prevention and Control. A Practical Guide

DETR 2000. The Air Quality Strategy

Kyoto Protocol 1997

Further information

DETR 2001. Climate Change: The UK Programme

DETR 2000. Air Quality and Land Use Planning LAQM. G4

case example

Proposed Tall Building

The ES for a 41-storey major office headquarters building in London included consideration of the following micro-climatic effects:

- effects on pedestrian level wind
- effects of wind pressures on surrounding buildings
- the wind induced structural response of a nearby building
- effects on daylight and sunlight
- the effect of light reflecting off the building
- artificial lighting and light spillage
- shadow effects.

Regulators and consultees

Local Authority Environmental Health Department

Environment Agency

Air, Climate, Odour

Proposed Windfarm

The ES for a windfarm comprising 16 three-blade wind turbines, with a combined maximum output of 8 MW, reported that it would be expected to offset the emission of over 24,000 t of carbon dioxide, as well as saving the emission of around 350 t/year of acid rain gases.

Potential Effects

Air quality effects can arise during both construction and operation. During the construction phase, dust is likely to be a primary concern, albeit of a temporary nature. Construction traffic and plant may also release pollutants into the atmosphere, however, these emission sources are unlikely to result in significant long-term impacts.

Proposals for major developments such as for power stations, incinerators, chemical factories and oil refineries (projects which are usually Schedule 1 developments) can lead to concerns about significant air quality impacts during their operation. However, for many development types, the principal concern during operation is likely to relate to emissions from traffic. The significance of the impact will depend on the level of traffic generated by the development and the existing conditions.

Odour is not often a concern, but can be an issue in relation to developments such as wastewater treatment works, landfills, chemical plants, oil refineries, food processing factories and intensive farming units, such as pig farms. Particular attention should be paid to developments that might affect air quality management areas, as even small changes are likely to be considered significant.

As discussed above, consideration should also be given to climatic effects, at both the local and global scale.

Methodology

Baseline Studies

Gathering baseline air quality data can be an expensive exercise, therefore, it is best to use existing sources of data wherever possible. Air quality data is now readily available on the Internet at the UK National Air Quality Information Archive website. Local authorities can also provide data and this is increasingly also being made available on the Internet. Such data provides up to date information and also has the advantage of having been gathered over a number of years so it can be used to identify historical trends. It may have disadvantages however, since monitoring may not have been undertaken in the locations, or for the pollutants, of concern in the EIA. The local authority air quality review and assessment report will provide useful information on the air quality setting for the proposal and identify whether the development will be in or close to an air quality management area.

Where additional surveys are required, it is important to survey over a sufficient period since air quality can vary considerably over a short period of time. Variations can arise due to factors such as changes in wind direction, weather conditions and changes in traffic flow. Seasonal factors also play a part and should be borne in mind when assessing air quality data. In addition to considering the timing of the survey, it is also necessary to determine which pollutants will be surveyed, how and where. These decisions will be influenced by the characteristics of the development and the sensitivities of the receiving environment. Where it is necessary to monitor over a limited period, then the results should be put in perspective by making comparison with results for a nearby long-term site. This will demonstrate how representative the monitoring period is.

Further information

UK National Air Quality Information Archive website:
www.aeat.co.uk/netcen/airqual/index.html

The UK Air Quality Strategy sets objectives for the control of air pollutants as follows:

Protection of health	Protection of vegetation and ecosystems
■ benzene	■ nitrogen oxides
■ 1,3-butadiene	■ sulphur dioxide.
■ carbon monoxide	
■ lead	
■ nitrogen dioxide	
■ ozone	
■ particles (PM_{10})	
■ sulphur dioxide.	

The above list highlights the principal pollutants of concern. An EIA will not necessarily consider all of these but may also need to consider others such as carbon dioxide, methane and dioxins, depending on the nature of the development.

Once the data has been gathered, it can then be evaluated against the objectives set out in the Air Quality Strategy. In order to determine the impacts of the development, it is important to understand the quality of the receiving environment and its capacity to accept further pollutants.

Having established the existing baseline, it is necessary to predict what the baseline will be in the year of assessment. This includes careful consideration of which years of meteorological data to use. When predicting the future baseline, factors such as improvements in vehicle emissions should be taken into account, together with other developments that are proposed in the area that may give rise to significant air quality impacts.

If examining micro-climatic effects, data will need to be gathered regarding existing conditions, e.g. temperature, wind speed and direction, rainfall and shadowing. Where odour is to be assessed, existing sources of odour will need to be identified and odour levels assessed as appropriate.

Project Description

In describing the project it is important to highlight all potential sources of emissions to air during both construction and operation. Consideration should also be given to the impact of local sources on the development site, e.g. a food retail development next to an existing industrial source, or a proposed residential development next to a busy motorway. Sources will include traffic, plant and industrial processes. Information such as stack emissions, stack height and traffic generation will therefore need to be provided, as appropriate.

Impact Prediction and Significance

Predicting air quality impacts generally involves complex calculations and sophisticated computer modelling. Dispersion models can be used to

Key fact

Traffic Impact Assessment

Data generated as part of the Traffic Impact Assessment (TIA) will need to be appropriate for the air quality assessment. It is therefore important to discuss data requirements with the project managers and traffic consultants at an early stage. Without such discussion the TIA may generate data for locations, times of the day and years that are inappropriate for the air quality assessment as they are different types of study with different objectives

Further information

DETR 2000. Review and Assessment: Selection and use of Dispersion Models, LAQM. TG 3

Air, Climate, Odour

model industrial emissions, including odour. Such models require information about the stack, the type and rate of pollutants to be emitted, meteorological conditions, the local terrain and the proximity of buildings. As with any model, the data obtained is only as good as the data entered and it is important for the ES to provide details of all the inputs and assumptions made in carrying out the modelling so that the validity of the modelling can be examined.

For many projects, traffic is the principal source of air pollutants and in this instance a different approach to air quality prediction is required. The methodology set out by the Highways Agency in its Design Manual for Roads and Bridges (DMRB), Volume 11 is frequently used. The DMRB approach takes account of the number of vehicles, the proportion of Heavy-Duty Vehicles (HDVs), the distance from the road to the receptor, the speed of the vehicles and the effects of legislation on future emissions from vehicles. In certain circumstances, it may be appropriate to use more sophisticated models.

Whatever modelling is carried out, it will normally be necessary to add the predicted concentrations to the local background (see baseline discussion above). It is also likely to be necessary to validate the models, especially if the predicted concentrations are close to the objectives.

Having predicted air quality levels with the development in place, it is then necessary to evaluate the significance of the impact by comparing the predicted levels with the existing situation and the predicted baseline for the year of assessment. Air quality should also be assessed against the relevant air quality standards. Impacts can be said to be significant if the development leads to exceedance of air quality standards, objectives or guidelines. Impacts may also be considered significant if there would be a serious deterioration in air quality, even without exceeding an air quality standard.

The assessment of significance will also need to take into account the sensitivity of the receiving environment such as schools, hospitals and SSSIs. In the case of an impact in an air quality management area, even a very small increase is likely to be considered significant and compensatory measures may be required from the developer.

Effects on the microclimate can be examined through the use of models, either physical scale models of the development, or computer models. Models can be used to assess effects on, e.g. wind patterns, sunlight, and shadowing.

case example

Proposed Energy Recovery Facility

The ES for this proposal included an assessment of the potential responses of vegetation and wildlife to sulphur dioxide, nitrogen dioxide, dioxins, furans and particulates. The proposed ERF was located in close proximity to a SSSI, SPA, cSAC and Ramsar site. Particular attention was paid to potential impacts on sphagnum flora and lichens.

Mitigation

Examples of mitigation measures can be identified for each of the types of impact identified in this section.

Air Quality:
- Promote greater atmospheric dispersion by raising the stack height, increasing the velocity of emission, etc. (noting potential increased visual impact).
- Modify industrial processes to use cleaner fuels or burn fuels more efficiently.

- Improve quality of emissions through use of scrubbers.
- Control the amount of traffic generated by the development proposals.

Dust:
- Damping down of materials and unpaved areas using water sprays.
- Sheeting of lorries using the construction site.
- Washing the wheels of vehicles before they leave the site.
- Covering of temporary stockpiles with sheeting.
- Locating any temporary stockpiles away from sensitive locations.
- Regular use of a water-assisted dust sweeper on local roads to remove any material tracked out of the site.

Microclimate:
- Orientate buildings in such a way to avoid overshadowing of existing dwellings or other sensitive areas and to prevent creating wind canyons.
- Selection of building and surfacing materials to avoid an excessive build up of heat.

Global Climate:
- Use alternative technologies for providing heat and electricity, e.g. solar power, wind turbines.
- Insulate buildings and orientate them so as to reduce heating/air conditioning requirements.
- Encourage use of alternative forms of transport to the car, e.g. walking, cycling, public transport.

Sources of Information	
Type	*Source*
Air Quality Data	UK National Air Quality Information Archive, Local Authority Environmental Health Department, Meteorological Office
Energy conservation and efficiency	ETSU
Environmental Assessment of buildings	Building Research Establishment Environmental Assessment Method (BREEAM)

Key Features

- Air quality modelling is a complex process. The inputs and assumptions on which modelling is based should be explicit in the ES.
- Air quality impacts **may** need to be considered from the local to the global scale; from microclimatic changes through to transboundary pollution and global warming.

Air, Climate, Odour/
Cultural Heritage and
Material Assets

■ Air quality assessments are closely related to traffic assessments. Traffic assessments should provide the data required to assess emissions from vehicles; any measures proposed to reduce traffic generation will also have a positive effect on emissions.

■ Changes in air quality can have an impact on flora and fauna. Air quality specialists may need to work with ecologists in order to determine the potential impacts of a development.

■ In some circumstances, air quality data may be required by health specialists in order to undertake an EHIA of the proposed development.

3.9 Cultural Heritage and Material Assets

Introduction

The Regulations refer to the need to describe *'material assets, including the architectural and archaeological heritage'* if they are likely to be significantly affected by the development (Schedule 4 Part I). The Directive refers more simply to *'material assets and the Cultural Heritage'*. The phrase *'material assets'* is not well-defined and has caused some difficulty.

The University of Bath IEM Workbook suggests some examples:

■ property values
■ loss of trading income
■ severance of land ownership, particularly farmland
■ compulsory purchase at less than market price
■ sterilization of mineral resources.

Clearly the issue has to be remembered when scoping an EIA but, by definition, material assets frequently have an economic value and such issues and disputes are more customarily resolved by commercial transactions, land valuation tribunals, compulsory purchase orders and are not strictly a part of environmental impact. However where, for example, agricultural activity or mineral extraction is involved such issues should be addressed under the appropriate heading. Many schemes which potentially would sterilize mineral resources provide for their winning as part of the project programme (see Section 3.6).

Discussion

It has in fact become customary and common practice in EIA to focus on the effects on archaeology and wider cultural assets and so this section is entitled Cultural Heritage as coined in the Directive. Schedule 4 Part I refers also to the need to describe the range of emissions from the proposed development including vibration and the effects of vibration on architecture or archaeology should be given special attention (see Section 3.4).

The selection criteria for screening Schedule 2 development draws special attention to the environmental sensitivity of the geographical areas likely to be affected by the development *'having regard to the absorption capacity of landscapes of historical, cultural or archaeological significance'*.

Material assets

" *this is a very broad all encompassing category which could cover almost every physical or non-physical sector of the environment that could be said to have material value ... there is no commonly accepted meaning of the term* "

– University of Bath IEM, EIA Workbook 1995

---

case example

Testwood Lakes

The development of reservoirs in the floodplain of the River Test in Hampshire included the winning of sands and gravels from the site *prior* to construcion.

The Regulations also interpret 'sensitive area' as:

- a property appearing on the World Heritage List of the 1972 UNESCO Convention for the Protection of the World Cultural and Natural Heritage
- a scheduled monument within the meaning of the Ancient Monuments and Archaeological Areas Act 1979.

The DoE 1995 Good Practice Guide clarifies matters by treating cultural heritage and material assets as a single topic area. The term is described as embracing history, archaeology, architecture and urban design and includes aspects not limited to material and economic value but extends them to human activities, ideas and spiritual and intellectual attitudes. Areas with particular associations with works of art or literature could well fall into this category.

The checklist of matters to be considered for inclusion in an ES in the Guide to Procedures (DETR 2000) suggest the following:

- **Information describing the Site and its environment:** Architectural and historic heritage, archaeological sites and features and other material assets. Heritage coasts, conservation areas, listed buildings, scheduled ancient monuments and designated areas of archaeological importance.
- **Assessment of effects on buildings and man-made features:** Effects of the development on buildings, the architectural and historic heritage, archaeological features, and other human artefacts, e.g. through pollutants, visual intrusion, vibration (the effects on land include agriculture and mineral resource sterilization).
- **Mitigating measures:** These might include recording of archaeological sites and measures to safeguard historic buildings or sites.

Regulators and Consultees

Initial consultation should be with the relevant county archaeologist. While not specifically listed in the Regulations as a consultee for EIA matters, the statutory consultee for heritage issues in England is English Heritage. Where development is likely to affect the site of a scheduled monument or any garden or park of special historic interest which is registered in accordance with Section 8C of the Historic Buildings and Ancient Monuments Act 1953 (register of gardens) and which is classified as Grade I or Grade II* the consultee is English Heritage (the Historic Buildings and Monuments Commission for England). Development of land in Greater London which involves the demolition, in whole or part, or the material alteration of a listed building should also be referred to English Heritage.

Development within three kilometres of Windsor Castle, Windsor Great Park, or Windsor Home Park, or within 800 m of any other royal palace or park, which might affect the amenities (including security) of that palace or park requires consultation with the Secretary of State for Media, Culture and Sport.

For listed buildings outside London applications are made through the local planning authority. The principal point of contact for advice and

Regulators and consultees
English Heritage, Local authority: County Archaeologist, Conservation Officer

*Cultural Heritage and
Material Assets*

guidance on the procedures is usually the Conservation Officer within the planning department.

For information regarding cultural heritage features, local authorities will often consult the National Trust, the Society for the Protection of Ancient Buildings, the Civic Trust, the Garden History Society, the Victorian Society, the Twentieth Century Society (formerly the Thirties Society) and will be able to advise on other national and local interest societies who may have particular information or may be able to advise on the significance, value and preservation of local features.

Potential Effects

Cultural heritage and those material or physical features representing it is irreplaceable and it is therefore essential that any remains or features are identified before development takes place. Where nationally important features (whether scheduled or not) and their settings are likely to be affected by proposed development there is a presumption in favour of their preservation *in situ*.

The possible effects on features of historic value can be summarized as follows:

- **Destruction:** e.g. demolition of listed building or disturbance of archaeology.
- **Visual or other intrusion:** e.g. impact on the character or setting of a building, conservation area or historic landscape which could include noise in a quiet setting.
- **Physical damage:** e.g. air pollution; water table fluctuations; vibration; recreational pressure for improved access; loss of fauna and flora especially for historic landscapes.

Methodology

The procedure for archaeological investigations (desk and field) is described in PPG 16 Archaeology and Planning which gives advice on handling archaeological remains under planning procedures. If the presence of such remains is suspected, planning consent may be withheld until sufficient information is made available to allow the local authority's archaeologists to formulate their advice. Provision of this information may involve commissioning historical map and documentary studies or the carrying out of site investigations. Further guidance is given in PPG 15 Planning and the Historic Environment. This sets out the arrangement for assessing other aspects of the cultural heritage landscape, principally the built environment: World Heritage Sites, Historic Parks and Gardens, Historic Battlefields, Listed Buildings and Conservation Areas.

Other key guidance

PPG 15 Planning and the Historic
        Environment

PPG 16 Archaeology and Planning

Baseline Studies

These should focus on the type of effect the various stages of the development could have and the potential cultural value of the site, if any. The study commences with a desk study guided by preliminary consultation with the local authority's archaeologist. The Institute of Field Archaeologists (IFA) Guidance sets out sources of archaeological information which should normally be included in desk-based studies including EIA. Sources which should be researched include:

National Monuments Record, held by English Heritage
This includes the National Archaeological Record for sites and monuments in England and the national library of aerial photographs as well as information on potential underwater sites or wrecks (Similar records for Scotland and Wales are held by their respective Commissions).

Sites and Monuments Records (SMRs) held by Local Authorities (England) Regional Archaeological Trusts (Wales) Regional and Island Councils (Scotland)
SMRs will normally contain a record of the known archaeological monuments (including scheduled monuments), sites and findspots together with references to further levels of information. The scope of SMRs varies: some routinely include listed buildings, post-WWII sites of interest, etc. while others take a much more restricted view of what constitutes the archaeological record. Any listing of known sites will be limited by the intensity of archaeological activity which has been undertaken, and the absence of recorded sites in certain areas does not necessarily indicate an absence of archaeological interest. SMRs do not usually comment on the importance of individual sites or areas, and expert guidance and advice is necessary. Of further help in this respect are areas identified by County Archaeologists as Areas of Archaeological Significance in local plans.

Listed Buildings
These are buildings or other features recognized as making an important contribution to the quality and character of the built environment. The listing is made by the Secretary of State at DEFRA and is usually available from the local planning authority.

Conservation Areas
These areas are designated in accordance with their special architectural or historical interest and their character and appearance. All trees within Conservation Areas are subject to Tree Preservation Orders. Conservation Areas are recorded on local plans produced by the local planning authority.

Historic Landscapes
These do not have statutory protection in their own right but may be part of designated areas, e.g. National Park, Area of Outstanding Natural Beauty (AONB), New Forest. They should be identified on local plans produced by the local planning authority. Statutorily protected landscapes are designated by the Countryside Agency who can provide further information. There are also non-statutory landscape designations, e.g. Areas of Great Historic Value (AGHV). Other factors which may define archaeologically or historically significant landscapes

Cultural Heritage and Material Assets

include clusters of sites forming archaeological landscapes, or field patterns incorporating boundaries which can be defined as being of historic significance in accordance with the criteria in the Hedgerow Regulations.

The Register of Parks and Gardens

The Register of Parks and Gardens of special historic interest is maintained by English Heritage and published in County volumes – the local planning authority will hold the relevant volume.

The Register of Historic Battlefields

The Register of Historic Battlefields in England is maintained by English Heritage.

Ordnance Survey

Early editions of Ordnance Survey and privately published maps are usually held in the County Record Office (who can advise on other useful sources) or reference library of the area concerned.

If the desk study and field walkover identifies the potential for a site of importance to the cultural heritage, further archive research or field investigation will be required. Field work which may include geophysical study, trenching or trial pits will be undertaken to a brief prepared in consultation with the local authority archaeologist.

Because PPG 16 and best practice requires a staged approach to archaeological assessment, it is possible that the desk study will result in a requirement for further levels of fieldwork prior to determination of the planning application. As this requirement cannot always be foreseen, there needs to be suitable allowance in timetable and budgets to cover for this.

Evaluation

Sites, monuments and other features are all graded (with the exception of battlefields) according to a set of criteria. As an example, for the scheduling of Ancient Monuments the following are used:

- period
- rarity
- documentation
- group value
- survival and condition
- fragility or vulnerability
- diversity
- potential.

These criteria also provide a useful framework for evaluating locally important features.

case example

Water main construction

Determining archaeological potential by means of desk-based study and/or field investigation before commencement is likely to significantly reduce the likelihood of finding important remains during construction. No matter what level of prior investigation is carried out, however, it is still possible that unexpected archaeological sites may be encountered and disturbed. Here a previously unknown 13th-century medieval pottery kiln discovered during pipe laying works, is excavated. Where such findings can be anticipated, investigation in advance of contractors' activities will allow sites to be more thoroughly investigated without risk to development programme and budget.

Photo by AC Archaeology

Mitigation

The principal method of mitigation for a feature of Cultural Heritage importance is to identify it at an early stage in the project planning process (via effective scoping) and to avoid damage or disturbance and leaving a suitable buffer zone around it. If features are in close proximity to a development site then protection should be provided during construction.

If disturbance cannot be avoided then provision for further levels of investigation and recording, possibly excavation, may be necessary. If the feature cannot be left where it was found, then removal and relocation to an alternative site or to a museum may be appropriate. In the case of visual intrusion affecting the character of a site then screening or other design measures should be considered. In urban situations construction design should preserve the deposits *in situ*.

Preservation *in situ*, either by avoiding the sensitive area or limiting works (e.g. depths) to avoid impact, will always be the favoured option. Some elements of the built environment, e.g. milestones can be moved. Where impacts are unavoidable, the notion of 'preservation by record' is enshrined in PPG 16. This may involve archaeological recording in advance of construction by means of archaeological excavation or other recording, or during the course of construction as part of an archaeological watching brief maintained during the relevant phases of the development. The course of action will depend on the likely importance of the archaeological remains affected, and will need to be undertaken to a specification agreed by the local authority archaeologist. It does need to be borne in mind that some developments may have a beneficial impact in the removal of clutter from historically important streetscapes or landscapes, opening up of views, or opportunities for restoration, e.g. of earthworks.

Where sites have potential but are otherwise of unknown quality an archaeological watching brief should be maintained by an experienced archaeologist during construction and for time to be allowed in the programme for recording and relocation of any finds. Enhancement of knowledge of the archaeological record may also be developed as a result of the site investigations, e.g. by providing access as an educational resource.

Key Features

■ Avoiding historic features and preservation *in situ* will always be the favoured mitigation option.

■ There is no commonly accepted meaning of the term 'material assets'.

■ Cultural heritage can include spiritual and intellectual attitudes as well as economic value.

■ Because archaeology is so often hidden from view, time must be allowed in the EIA programme for the unexpected.

■ A phased approach is required for archaeological assessment.

■ Cultural heritage is irreplaceable.

Further information

Institute of Field Archaeologists

Council for British Archaeology

Key fact

landscape includes consideration of
townscape and visual amenity

Key legislation & guidance

Countryside and Rights of Way Act 2000
Rural and Urban White Papers 2000
Hedgerow Regulations 1997
PPG7 The Countryside
PPG15 Planning and the Historic
Environment
CC 1993 Landscape Assessment Guidance
(under revision)
Countryside Agency Landscape Character
Assessment (in preparation)
Countryside Agency et al 2001 Quality of Life
Capital
Landscape Institute/IEA 1995 Guidelines for
Landscape and Visual Impact Assessment
(under revision)

3.10 Landscape

Introduction

If the landscape, townscape or visual amenity is likely to be significantly affected by the proposed development, then the EIA Regulations require a description of the baseline existing conditions, the likely significant effects and the measures envisaged to prevent, reduce or offset such adverse effects. It is important to note that the Regulations require attention to be paid to emissions of light in the description of the development and so night time effects should be addressed. (The Regulations refer to the term 'landscape' but good practice includes consideration of 'townscape' to refer to the urban environment and of visual amenity).

The selection criteria for screening Schedule 2 development draws special attention to the environmental sensitivity of the geographical areas likely to be affected by the development having regard to the absorption capacity of the natural environment including landscapes of historical, cultural or archaeological significance (see also 3.9 Cultural Heritage).

The Regulations include within the definition of sensitive areas the following:

- a National Park
- the Broads
- a World Heritage Site (UNESCO Convention for the Protection of the World Cultural and Natural Heritage)
- an area of outstanding natural beauty (AONB) designated as such by an order made by the Countryside Agency in England (or the Countryside Council for Wales in Wales) under the National Parks and Access to the Countryside Act 1949
- the New Forest Heritage Area.

The checklist of landscape matters to be considered for inclusion in an ES in the Guide to Procedures (DETR 2000) suggests the following:

Description of the site and its environment
Landscape and topography
National parks, areas of outstanding natural beauty (AONB), heritage coasts, regional parks, country parks and designated green belt

Assessment of effects on human beings, buildings and man-made features:
Visual effects of the development on the surrounding area and landscape and on buildings
Heritage, archaeological features and other human artefacts, e.g. through visual intrusion

Mitigating measures
Site planning and aesthetic measures such as:
Mounding
Design/colour
Landscaping
Tree planting
Assessment of the likely effectiveness of these measures

Discussion

Landscape, in broad terms, is about the relationship between people and places. Landscape impact assessment addresses the changes to places, and the perception of those changes by people, as a result of development. Such impacts are assessed through two separate, but closely related methodologies; landscape character impact assessment and visual impact assessment. Landscape character impact is considered through the understanding of the landscape resource. The landscape resource results from the way different components of the environment interact together and are perceived as:

- natural, including the influences of geology, soils, climate, flora and fauna, and
- cultural/social, including, the historical and contemporary impact of land use, settlement, enclosure and other human interventions.

Visual impact is considered through the study of the visual resource and the receptors who experience that resource.

Landscape character assessment can make a contribution to the aims of sustainable development in terms of environmental protection and the prudent use of resources. Landscape character assessment is defined as:

- the characterisation process which includes mapping, classifying and describing landscape character and making judgements based on character to inform decisions.

Regulators and Consultees

The statutory consultee for landscape issues in England is the Countryside Agency. However, this body is principally concerned with designated sites such as AONBs and the onus for guiding determination of landscape matters is more likely to fall on the landscape officer for the relevant local planning authority. County planning authorities are the consultee for development in National Parks where the National Park Board is the planning authority.

Development affecting registered historic gardens or parks requires consultation with English Heritage.

Other consultees with an interest in landscape matters include the Environment Agency who has a duty to consider the effects of development on the landscape, especially in respect of river valleys, and the CPRE who, in particular, have initiated a Dark Skies Campaign, and the National Trust. Parish councils, local residents and communities will be particularly concerned with landscape change in their locality.

Potential Effects

Direct effects on the landscape can occur through removal, alteration or addition of key features and defining characteristics. This may be through a change in landform, built form or landcover, as well as change in the prevailing management regime. Such changes may result in a loss of status in terms of national, regional or local designations.

Key fact

Landscape Character Assessment is not a tool to resist change – its role is to ensure that change does not undermine what is characteristic or valued about a particular landscape

- Countryside Agency, 2000

Regulators and consultees

Countryside Agency

Local Authority: planning, landscape and conservation

National Parks Authority

Broads Authority

English Heritage

National Trust

Garden History Society

CPRE

Open Spaces Society

Civic Trust

case example

Landraising scheme, Berkshire

A landraising scheme for waste disposal was proposed in a relatively remote location in Berkshire. Despite thorough formal consultation which elicited very little in terms of opinions of the proposal, the promoters were somewhat surprised when over 200 people turned up to a public meeting to voice their opposition. The scheme was even reported in a national tabloid newspaper. In the face of such concern the scheme was withdrawn.

Landscape

The visual impact is a function of how visible a development is in its landscape context and the magnitude and range of this visibility. This is likely to affect those with views to the proposed development most or those who value the landscape for particular cultural reasons. Impacts can include not only the development itself but also emissions e.g. steam plumes, or indirect effects e.g. traffic movement. The potential of visual impact to harm the recreational use of landscape should also be remembered. However the effect on overall visual amenity can be one of enhancement as well as degradation.

Methodology

Landscape and visual effects have to be considered on the landscape resource itself (both natural and man made) and on the way landscape is perceived by the public.

Much of landscape impact assessment is based on professional judgement and it is important that the methodologies, terminology and techniques used should be accurately explained and described and any limitations of the assessment clearly identified. A structured approach, recording findings at stages of the assessment should be maintained.

Impartiality should be maintained as far as possible distinguishing between facts and judgments; the worst case and precautionary principle should be applied especially with respect to seasonal variations.

Since there are two types of impact, two separate but related methodologies are used. recording findings at stages of the assessment should be maintained.

Impartiality should be maintained as far as possible distinguishing between facts and judgments; the worst case and precautionary principle should be applied especially with respect to seasonal variations.

1. Landscape Character Assessment. This, essentially, is a study based on the existing landscape character of a locality or district. Frequently such studies will already have been carried out for the purposes of designation or identification of particular areas and their recognition in local development plans. It is important to clearly define the geographical extent of the studies from the beginning and should at least cover the whole contextual setting of the development (including construction as well as operational phases). The purpose is to identify areas of countryside with **common and defining** characteristics:

e.g. rolling pastoral (agricultural) landscape with shallow river valleys and heather or conifer plantations on the hill tops

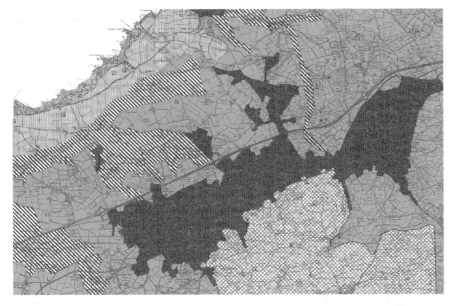

Granite Uplands

Urban

Agricultural Plateau

Steep Sided River Valleys

Coastal

Landscape Character Illustration

Landscape character assessments require both objective recording (as in the example above) and a **subjective** valuation based on our appreciation of a particular landscape type:

e.g. a comfortable, contained landscape but in which the regularity of the plantations is prominent.

Needless to say, landscape assessments need to be richly illustrated with photographs, sketches, maps or archive material. The Countryside Agency Assessment approach takes three stages:

(a) Landscape description
This is based on field survey (baseline study) and describes what is there i.e.

■ landform – this is the physical structure and is related principally to the underlying geology and consequent function of topography, rivers, soils and landform processes.

■ Landcover - this relates to vegetation, and land use (such as arable or pasture, agriculture or urban uses).

■ Landscape elements - these include hedgerows, buildings, skylines and lines of slope, cultural associations, biodiversity and settlement patterns.

(b) Landscape classification
As noted above, this may have already been provided by a local authority, the Countryside Agency, or others. The principal purpose is to identify areas of similar character and defining characteristics or features and then to see how they relate to each other and how robust certain areas to any proposed changes in use or management would be. As the Countryside Commission stated "landscape is more than just the sum of its parts" (CC 423) so it is necessary to describe how individual elements relate to each other.

Landscape

Quality of Life Capital (QoL)

QoL Capital has been developed from the landscape character and environmental captial methods of assessment. It is a technique for:

- Identifying why something, such as a place or a building, might matter for people's quality of life
- Identifying the various benefits (and any disbenefits) of the place or building, and then determining the importance of these various benefits
- Assessing whether, and if so how, these benefits could be substituted, if lost or damaged

Criteria are used for ascribing importance to the features or situations which concern them. Environmental criteria include:

- Distinctiveness
- Quality
- Rarity
- Representativeness
- Setting/context
- Historical continuity
- Recorded history
- Accessibility
- Popularity

(c) Landscape evaluation

This is an assessment of the quality and value of the landscape summarizing why it is or is not important. The Countryside Commission (CCP 423) have produced Field Survey Sheets which may be utilized for the above process.

At this stage it is essential to take the opinions of residents into account and to reach a consensus as to what is important and why.

2. Visual Impact Assessment. This determines the area from which a proposed development may be seen (the Zone of Visual Influence, ZVI).

(a) Zone of Visual Influence

This is established by a combination of desk study using Ordnance Survey maps and contours and/or a digital terrain model computer programme, and field survey which confirms the findings of the desk study. The field survey is also used to obtain photographs using typical eye level view to illustrate the actual nature of the view. The desk study ZVI is refined by the field study which can establish that intervening features such as woodland can limit the visual envelope.

(b) Visual Impact

This entails using a number of discrete viewpoints which may be agreed with the Landscape Officer of the local authority or the Countryside Agency in advance. They should be chosen to represent particular key views which may be sensitive to change or designated areas from which policy may dictate that views should not be changed to any great extent. Distinction should be made between public and private views. Views at different seasons and including day and night time vistas should be used. Key receptors and their sensitivity should be recorded. The impacts have to be illustrated and this can be done by 'before and after' sketches but their representation is most successfully achieved by using photomontages for which considerable accuracy is required. Scale models can also be used but they tend to accentuate 'birds eye' views which of course are unrepresentative of the 'normal view'.

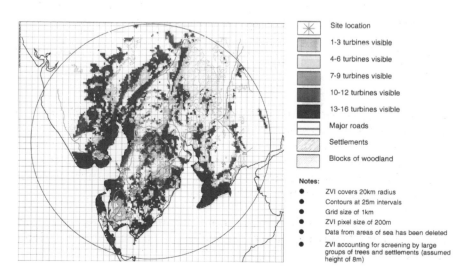

Example of computer generated ZVI

Legend:
- Site location
- 1-3 turbines visible
- 4-6 turbines visible
- 7-9 turbines visible
- 10-12 turbines visible
- 13-16 turbines visible
- Major roads
- Settlements
- Blocks of woodland

Notes:
- ZVI covers 20km radius
- Contours at 25m intervals
- Grid size of 1km
- ZVI pixel size of 200m
- Data from areas of sea has been deleted
- ZVI accounting for screening by large groups of trees and settlements (assumed height of 8m)

3. Evaluation. Once the landscape and visual resource which may be affected by the proposed development, together with any recorded designated areas or areas covered by landscape policies, has been identified, the impacts and their significance can be predicted. Impacts may include the loss of particular elements or changes in character and views, and are always related to existing quality, sensitivity and enhancement potential. The significance of change is assessed by identifying impacts on the landscape character of an area or locality, the landscape resource and the visual resource.

Significance criteria include national, regional or local importance, sensitivity to change, rarity, uniqueness, representativeness, cultural association and effects on designated areas. The effects on designated areas should include a consideration of the importance of any change.

To an extent the question of 'significance' will be a judgement but it is possible to quantify distance of views, numbers of people affected and whether they are residents or visitors. Such information can initially be gleaned from desk study but can be enhanced by means of questionnaires or public exhibitions. Any subjective opinions should be clearly stated as such.

The evaluation should take into account the time taken for any mitigation such as tree planting to take effect and for any predicted changes which will take place, e.g. change of management regime, irrespective of whether the proposed development proceeds.

Mitigation

The principal aim of landscape mitigation is to 'design out' negative impacts and requires close liaison within the team from an early stage. In other words, 'mitigation' starts at the commencement of the design process including decisions relating to alternative site options. The opportunities to explore landscape enhancement options, especially where these will contribute to local authority aspirations for an area should be considered.

Frequently, landscape design or management proposals may be perceived as a restoration of, or improvement to, the existing landscape. Even so, such restoration may involve impacts, e.g. dust, temporary soil storage, and such measures adopted to mitigate this should be described.

Care should be taken during consultation to ensure that what may appear to be 'derelict' landscapes are not actually valued for local or national reasons.

In developing the mitigation strategy it is essential to set out the design objectives e.g. screen, break line of sight, respect designations, and should be based on the landscape character and visual context of the area in which the development site is located. Mitigation for such effects can be approached by using the mitigation hierarchy storage, and such measures adopted to mitigate this should be described.

Care should be taken during consultation to ensure that what may appear to be 'derelict' landscapes are not actually valued for local or national reasons.

case example

Blaenavon

In the 1980s, schemes were prepared for the restoration of the derelict landscape of previous open cast coal workings. These schemes never progressed and in 2000 the area was included in the Blaenavon World Heritage Site as representing a historic landscape and evidence of the activities for which the area is important.

Landscape

In developing the mitigation strategy it is essential to set out the design objectives e.g. screen, break line of sight, respect designations, and should be based on the landscape character and visual context of the area in which the development site is located. Mitigation for such effects can be approached by using the mitigation hierarchy:

Avoidance
■ Achieved by locating elsewhere, alternative location within the development site, or overall design. If alternatives are considered but rejected, the reasons should be reported in the ES.

Reduction
■ This reduces the landscape and visual impact to a point where a scheme which, whilst apparent, may not adversely affect the landscape or visual resource. Measures include screening by using existing vegetation or topography, new planting or bunds, design of structures, their colour or finish. At all times, respecting the existing landscape pattern or structure maximises the effectiveness of such measures.

Remediation
■ This includes new earth modelling, replacement of lost features or new planting.

Enhancement
■ Offsite planting or other measures, e.g. river restoration.

The effectiveness of the mitigation will need to be monitored and measures to rectify any shortfalls identified and committed to in the ES. For example a local authority may wish to ensure that proposed screening measures are implemented and are effective by regular monitoring. Landscape does not reach its maximum effectiveness overnight and so management of planting is an essential requirement for the success of such mitigation.

Summary of Mitigation at Stages of Development

Pre-development	Advanced planting to assist screening Earth moving and formation of screen bunds
Design stage	Incorporate existing landscape features, e.g. water features, hedgerows, woodland belts, into scheme design Grouping of buildings to minimize intrusion Design to reflect local architectural character or form, e.g. farm buildings or create new complementary features New planting areas to screen important views Use colours and materials to reduce prominent of buildings Introduce new landscape features consistent with local landscape character, e.g. wetland habitats

| Construction and operation | Protect and maintain existing landscape features Use low-level shrouded lighting consistent with security requirements |
| Restoration | Clear the site and restore or recreate habitats or woodland using local indigenous plant species. |

Sources of Information

Type	Source
Character Map of England	Countryside Agency
Natural Areas	English Nature
Countryside Stewardship	Countryside Agency
AONB Landscape guides	Countryside Agency
Landscape Character Areas of Great Landscape Value (or similar)	Local Authority
Rights of Way	Local Authority
Common Land	Land Registry
Environmentally Sensitive Areas	DEFRA (ESAs)
Soils	Soil Survey of England and Wales
Geology	British Geological Society
Historic Features	Ordnance Survey and private mapmakers
Aerial photographs	Ordnance Survey and private suppliers

Key features

- Landscape takes time to mature and mitigation proposals must make clear the time taken to be effective.
- Landscape effects include effects on the character of the landscape and on the way it is perceived by the public.
- Landscape effects can interact with historic features and ecology.
- Landscape is often the principal change perceived by the public as a result of development.

Further information

Chartered Landscape Institute

Institute of Leisure and Amenity Management

English Heritage 2000 Yesterdays World, Tomorrows Landscape

National Trust 2000 Archaeology and the Historic Environment: Historic Landscape Survey Guidelines

CCW Guide to Best Practice in Seascape Assessment

Institute of Lighting Engineers 1997 Guidance Notes for the Reduction of Light Pollution

Countryside Commission 1997 Lighting in the Countryside: Towards Good Practice

3.11   Planning Context

Introduction

Any proposed development, whether it requires planning consent or whether it falls under other onshore consent regimes, will be subject to a range of planning policies relating to the locality. There may also be statutory designations and standards on and for the development site and its environs; these have been referred to in the previous sections. Since planning authorities are required to determine planning applications in accordance both with international and government guidance and with the development plan for the area, such applications will generally be accompanied by a supporting planning statement which will attempt to demonstrate compliance, or degree of compliance, with the applicable policies. It is not a requirement of the EIA Regulations that such compliance is repeated in an ES.

However, the *Guide to Procedures* (DETR 2000) does advise that the Policy Framework should be described. Any description should, therefore, demonstrate how such policies have been taken into account in formulating the project: frequently a developer will examine the relevant local plan to identify a range of sites where the proposed development would comply with policies. If this process is carried out it is appropriate for it to be described in a section in the ES on Alternatives.

In considering various international, national and local policies and guidance it is useful to:

- state the status of the document (e.g. date, whether adopted or non-statutory guidance)
- highlight key issues relevant to the development
- explain how the documents have been taken into account.

The planning review is not a 'promotional' element of the ES but should be balanced and impartial.

Assessment of Effects

This requires a description of the existing land uses of the site and its surroundings – which broadly may be recorded in the local plan documents, including landscape descriptions and assessments. Comparison with the land-use requirements – which include, e.g. temporary uses or access arrangements – of the project allows conclusions to be drawn by the regulatory authority officers.

Of particular interest will be:

- loss of agricultural land
- land allocated in the Local Plan for specific uses especially where these do not comply with the use being sought. Employment and residential land is held at a premium
- effects on adjacent sensitive land uses, e.g. residential, health care, educational (in some instances a proposed land use will be incompatible with those existing on adjacent sites)
- sterilization of mineral resources
- the site's relationship to the settlement boundary or limit of development, and whether it is a previously occupied 'brownfield' site.

---

case example

Proposed Windfarm

This proposal was accompanied by an ES and supported by a Planning Statement. The Planning Statement discussed the need for wind energy, the strength of UK policy in favour of wind energy and then identified national and local policy documents and debated their particular relevance to the proposal. It concluded with a discussion of the policy issues: Policy AT identifies Access Tracks as a key issue. The support statement explained how the impacts of the access tracks would be minimized and how the granting of planning permission would not breach Policy AT.

case example

Football Stadium development

The Land Use Planning/Policy Context of this ES very briefly identified the land-use designation for the site and its surroundings such as Conservation Areas, Listed Buildings, SSSIs. This was followed with a review of relevant policy documents: National (PPGs) Regional (RPGs) and Local (the Development Plan and Conservation Area briefs) and focused on the principles which these sought to apply as being relevant to the proposed development. For example Policy WD requires that new residential development should provide facilities for recycling waste. At no point did the ES attempt to 'promote' the development.

Mitigation

In this context mitigation is the selection of a site whose proposed use in the development plan is compatible with that proposed by the developer. If the development, while otherwise acceptable, would sterilize minerals then the prior mining of those minerals may well be an option to mitigate the otherwise negative impact.

Sources of Information

- International Treaties and Conventions
- Planning Policy Guidance
- Mineral Planning Guidance
- Regional Planning Guidance
- County and Unitary Plans
- Local Development Plans
- Minerals Local Plans
- Waste Local Plans
- Issues papers
- Area development or conservation briefs
- Other Supplementary Planning Guidance.

Review of Planning History

It is also helpful to consider the planning history of the site and, if appropriate, adjacent sites. While interpreting previous decisions would principally be of use in site selection and prior to submitting a planning application, it can also be used to demonstrate how the development's design had been modified or its impacts mitigated in order to overcome what had previously been identified as key issues.

3.12 Integration and Synthesis

Introduction

The effects that a proposed development project may have on any one environmental topic are likely to have effects on other topics and yet the interactions between them are rarely specifically addressed in EIAs. This may be associated with the lack of a standard method for assessing impact interactions but it is often related to the practice of addressing each significant environmental topic separately in the ES. Scoping should identify potential interactions, although cumulative and indirect effects, as well as interactions, may also become apparent as the EIA progresses.

The EIA Regulations require a description of the interactions between effects, and an assessment of indirect and cumulative effects – these are often associated with interactions. For example, effluent discharges to a watercourse may affect flow regimes and water quality such that a habitat may be affected; traffic and air quality and noise are clearly inter-related with each other and they affect the well-being and health of local communities and wildlife. The consideration of interactions is an essential part of cumulative effects (impact) assessment (CE(I)A).

case example

Wastewater Treatment Works

The ES for this proposal included a Policy Context section. This looked briefly at the International Treaties (e.g. Ramsar Convention, EC Directives) National Legislation and Guidance (e.g. Environmental Protection Act 1990, UK Strategy for Sustainable Development, Circulars and PPGs) Development Plan Context (Structure Plan, Minerals and Waste Local Plan and Borough Local Plans). In all cases it identified the particular status of the documents and drew out the relevant sections for the proposal. However, it also included a summary paragraph which attempted to demonstrate how the proposal was in accord with the policy context. This is acceptable, but phrases such as 'broadly in accordance with the provisions' might lead the reader to suspect (rightly or wrongly) that there are some elements which may not be in accordance with policy.

The EIA Regulations require a description in the ES of the **inter-relationships** between environmental factors likely to be significantly affected by the proposed development. When considering effects of the development on the environment, the description of effects should cover:

- direct and indirect
- secondary
- cumulative
- short, medium and long term
- permanent and temporary
- positive and negative.

Key fact

The integrated assessment of effects including direct, indirect and cumulative, together with interactions, contributes towards sustainable development

Integration and Synthesis

As far as possible, the interactions between potential effects should be considered as part of the impact assessments carried out for each environmental topic and reported separately for clarity in the ES. Interactions between effects should also be considered for each stage of the project: construction, operation/occupation, and decommissioning/restoration.

It can be useful for the reader if the ES summarizes cumulative effects and interactions, intended mitigation measures, and any residual impacts in a final short section. This approach unifies the various environmental topics thus acknowledging the complex inter-relationships amongst environmental systems. It is inappropriate for an ES to reach conclusions as such, since the decision making is carried out by others. The section may rather summarize impacts assessment and interactions, together with mitigation and how it will be achieved. Such an integrated and holistic approach follows principles of sustainability.

> **guiding principle**
>
> Sustainability and sustainable development should not be confused – they are different

"

Environmental impacts are at the core of sustainability concerns

– Sadler 1999

"

Definitions
- *Impact*: a change to the environment attributable to the proposed development.
- *Effect*: the result of an impact on a receptor or resource.
- *Direct*: *Effect* an effect arising from an impact attributable to an element or an activity of the project.
- *Indirect*: *Effect* an effect which does not directly impact on a receptor or resource.
- *Secondary*: *Effect* an effect which may arise as a consequence of another effect, often between different environmental topics.
- *Cumulative*: *Effect* these may arise from
    - interactions between different effects at the same location
    - interactions of different effects over time
    - additive or multiple impacts over time or space
    - effects of a number of developments.
- *Short/Medium/Long Term*: there are no standard categories but typical timescales may be 0–2/2–5/5–10 years. The environmental agencies are thinking in terms of 30 or 50 years; some LAs are thinking more than the 10 years of a development plan in order to comply with SA requirements.
- *Permanent Effect*: an effect which is irreversible or likely to persist for the life of the development.
- *Temporary Effect*: an effect which is limited either because the impact ceases or because the environment can assimilate it.

Cumulative Effects Assessment (CEA)

Cumulative effects of human activities, such as climate change and loss of biodiversity, have led to notable scientists predicting that environmental deterioration may be reaching critical thresholds with irreversible loss of natural systems. The predication of impacts affecting the global system are very difficult to estimate at the project level and such matters may be better dealt with at the strategic plan and policy level through Strategic Environmental Assessment (SEA). There is government encouragement (PPG 12) in the UK to carry out Sustainability Appraisals (SAs) and this will be reinforced when the EU directive on SEA is implemented.

Cumulative effects can arise from actions and processes as follows:
- additive
- interactive
- sequential
- multiple
- synergistic
- threshold exceedence.

Cumulative effects are the total effect on a given resource, ecosystem and human community of all actions taken, past, present and foreseeable future; they rarely correlate with political and administrative boundaries. Cumulative effects also come from existing activities, e.g. emissions and resource use from commerce and industry, transport movements. Therefore, CEA is perhaps better suited to assessing effects over wider spatial, e.g. at global, national, regional and sub-regional scales, and temporal boundaries than just a single project. Circular 02/99 states that CEA applies to the specific development and the responsibility for determining the cumulative impacts of a proposal in combination with other existing or proposed "developments" is that of the LPA. This assessment is based on information provided by developers. CEA and considerations of interactions demonstrate an holistic and integrated approach which contributes towards the objectives of sustainable development.

Cumulative effects can result from multiple pathways and can impact on both bio-physical and socio-economic resources and systems. These effects may be significant even though the individual effects may be insignificant when assessed separately. There is no standard method for CEA in the UK, however, there is comprehensive guidance elsewhere, e.g. from the EU, Canada and the USA. CEAs typically build upon existing methods and approaches in EIA; a useful aspect is the consideration of VECs. In the UK reliance is often put on professional judgement and expert opinion.

> **CEA methods include:**
> - Questionnaires, interviews and panels
> - Checklists
> - Matrices
> - Networks and systems diagrams
> - Modelling
> - Trends analysis
> - Overlay mapping and GIS
> - Carrying Capacity
> - Ecosystem analysis
> - Economic Impact Analysis
> - Social Impact Assessment
> - US Council on Environmental Quality 1997.

Sustainability and Sustainable Development

Sustainable Development (SD) now underpins the UK land-use planning system and government has stated (A Better Quality of Life, 1999) that policy will take into account 10 guiding principles:

- putting people at the centre
- taking a long-term perspective
- taking account of costs and benefits
- creating an open and supportive economic system
- combating poverty and social exclusion
- respecting environmental limits
- the precautionary principle
- using scientific knowledge
- transparency, information, participation and access to justice
- making the polluter pay.

Valued Ecosystem Component (VEC)

VECs are used in CEA and they represent any part of the environment that is considered important by the developer, public, scientists or government involved in the assessment process. Importance may be determined on the basis of cultural values or scientific knowledge/concern

Further information

EC 1999 Guidelines on the Assessment of Indirect and Cumulative Impacts as well as Impact Interactions. www.europa.eu.int

Canadian Environmental Assessment Agency 1999 Canadian Effects Assessment Practitioners Guide. www.ceaa.gc.ca

US Council on Environmental Quality 1997 Considering Cumulative Effects Under the National Environmental Policy Act. www.epa.gov

Canter L 1999 Cumulative Effects Assessment in Petts 1999 Handbook of Environmental Impact Assessment

The Royal Commission on Environmental Protection is preparing a report on Environmental Planning which considers issues including:

- environmental sustainability
- cumulative effects
- boundaries
- integration or co-ordination? – the relationship between landuse planning and pollution control.

www.rcep.org.uk

Integration and Synthesis

It may be argued that sustainability is about whether or not to develop, whereas sustainable development presumes that development will progress. Nonetheless, environmental sustainability is likely to become more important as the principles of sustainability are incorporated into development plans and programmes through PPG 12 and SAs and the forthcoming requirements of the EU SEA Directive, which will then have an effect on EIA.

Environmental sustainability is concerned with the regenerative and assimilative capacities of natural systems. The EIA Directive and Regulations require consideration of *'the … regenerative capacity of natural resources in the area; and the absorption capacity of the natural environment, … '* indicating clear links between EIA and sustainability.

Sustainability principles and concepts tend to follow one of two basic systems:

- Based on economic valuations of 'capital' stocks that should be passed on from one generation to the next.
- Based on socio-ecological systems which consider that human activities and resources usage should be within the range of natural cycles; this will need changes in social values and behaviour, e.g. to reduce the use of fossil fuel and keep within the use of renewable resources.

The earlier concept of Natural Capital used by English Nature has now been developed into Quality of Life Capital (CAG for English Nature, English Heritage, Countryside Agency and Environment Agency 2000), sponsored by the environmental agencies; it may be useful to assess the significance and interactions of environmental factors in EIA. The QoL Capital approach aims to identify what is important to a community and why. The Environment Agency is developing a threshold capacity approach which seeks to assess environmental sustainability and offer options for development (Carroll *et al.* 2002).

Sustainability Appraisal methods have evolved from SEA methods and may be used on development plans and for locational choices for development. These methods tend to be based on checklists of criteria against which progress towards sustainability/sustainable development can be assessed. The inter-relationships with EIA are likely to be addressed in the section of the ES which considers the planning context.

Objectives for Sustainable Development

- Social progress which recognizes the needs of everyone
- Effective protection of the environment
- Prudent use of natural resources
- Maintenance of high and stable levels of economic growth and employment
- UK Strategy for Sustainable Development, 1999

A better quality of life for everyone, now and for generations to come

– DETR 1999

Key fact

Sustainability and sustainable development are often used interchangeably but they are different

Key fact

EIA has a role to play in promoting sustainable construction as an element of mitigation.

Further information

DETR 1999 Proposals for a Good Practice Guide on Sustainability Appraisal of Regional Planning Guidance

Barton *et al.* 2002 Shaping neighbourhoods for health, sustainability and community

SOLACE, IdeA & LGA 1999 Best Value and Sustainability Checklist

DETR 2000 A Strategy for more Sustainable Construction

The UK Round Table on Sustainable Development recommended in its final report (2000) that the new Sustainable Development Commission should consider specific problems including '*inappropriate trade-offs, e.g. between environmental assets and economic gains from development proposals*'

> **Key Criteria for Environmental Sustainability Assessment**
>
> - Energy
> - Air
> - Water
> - Land and soils/food production
> - Open/green space
> - Amenity and recreation
> - Biodiversity and ecological networks
> - Pedestrian accessibility to local facilities
> - Public transport accessibility to jobs and centres
> - Aesthetic and cultural heritage
> - Infrastructure capacity
> - Sustainable construction materials
> - Sustainable waste management

Chapter 4

Development Types

Environmental Impact Assessment (EIA) is site-specific and the extent of potential impacts is dependent on the quality and characteristics of the receiving environment. However, development types tend to have characteristics also and these may suggest typical environmental impacts. This chapter is presented in checklist format for easy reference and lists key potential impacts, mitigation, monitoring, environmental management and further guidance for a range of development types. It also draws attention to the opportunities for environmental enhancement from development proposals.

4.1 Introduction

A number of development types drawn from the principal sectors of activity in the UK are addressed in this chapter. For each, the key characteristics of the development are listed, together with the legal requirement for EIA. The main scope of the EIA is indicated as a checklist of issues/terms of reference. This is only intended as a guide since the actual scope for any one EIA will be determined through the scoping exercise and will be site-specific. The likely impacts are shown with potential mitigation options: examples are indicated but there will be many more creative solutions to resolving potential environmental problems. Key legislation, guidance and further sources of information are listed.

guiding principle

EIA is site-specific

Within the context of environmental studies, development is often seen as detrimental to the environment. However, development can offer opportunities for environmental enhancement. Government policy supports the principle that it is reasonable to expect developers to contribute towards the cost of infrastructure – and this may include environmental benefits. It is essential for developers that this is considered early in project planning.

4.2 Characteristics of Projects

Every Environmental Statement (ES) should provide a full factual description of the project. Developers are also now required by the 1999 EIA Regulations to include an outline of the main alternative approaches to the proposed development and the main reasons for their choice. (There will be some developments for which there are no meaningful alternatives.)

The EIA Regulations require that the characteristics of projects must be considered having regard to:

- the size of the project
- the use of natural resources
- the risk of accidents and hazardous materials
- the cumulation with other projects
- the production of waste
- pollution and nuisances.

Characteristics of Projects

The Screening and Scoping stages of the EIA process will have described the project to an increasing degree. The level of detail required for the final ES is as follows:

Project Description

- Site setting and context of development:
  - general description of the proposed site location to include topography, catchment, land use and transport.
- Purpose and physical characteristics of the development:
  - area of site at all phases of the project including temporary contractors' compounds or laydown areas and access
  - design and size of buildings, structures, roads, landscaping, utilities.
- Project features should include all stages:
  - construction
  - operation/occupation
  - decommissioning
  - restoration.
- Operational characteristics of the development:
  - traffic (private, delivery, occupiers) generated
  - employees, visitors, residents, occupiers including construction workers
  - type and volume of materials, energy and resources used
  - frequency and duration of intrusive activities
  - energy consumption or production
  - emissions by type, quantity and quality – water, air, soil, noise, vibration, light, heat, radiation
  - residues such as wastes and methods of treatment – recycling, reuse.
- Alternatives: sites, processes, options.

The description should make full use of maps, figures, drawings, sketches or photomontages to illustrate the proposed development.

4.3 Minerals Extraction

Characteristics of Minerals Extraction Projects

- Risk of pollution, accident and nuisances.
- Temporary use of the land.
- Restoration commitment essential and long term.
- Commitment to an Environmental Management Plan (EMP) important.
- Opportunities for environmental, recreational and amenity enhancement for local communities.
- Alternatives limited since minerals can only be exploited where they are found.

Scope of EIA

The main considerations for minerals extraction are the scale of the development, emissions to air, discharges to water, risk of accident, and transport. Depending on the type of minerals development, environmental issues typically include visual intrusion, noise, dust, discharges to water, ecology, risk of accident and transport.

Mining, especially opencast, is very much a temporary use of the land and its resources; landscape architects have used the term 'landscape on loan' to describe (or perhaps downplay) its potential effects above ground. Therefore, the temporary nature of impacts are as important as the permanent or 'on restoration' proposals.

Because of the long-term nature of these temporary impacts, environmental management is of particular importance and the mining and extraction industry has in recent years led the field in its practical application. Since the exploitation of minerals is only temporary, mitigation must focus on restoration proposals.

Since minerals can only be exploited where they are found, alternative sites are not an option. However, alternative routings for traffic, and alternative process and infrastructure location still apply. (Renewal of Minerals Permissions (ROMPs) are subject to EIA for registration and review – EIA Regulations as amended 2000.)

Key Consultees

- Local Authorities: planning, highways, conservation, environmental health
- Minerals Planning Authority
- Environment Agency
- Conservation, Heritage and community groups
- Coal Authority
- Department for Environment, Food and Rural Affairs
- Health and Safety Executive
- English Nature
- English Heritage
- Countryside Agency.

EIA Regulations Projects Schedule

Schedule 1

Quarries and Opencast	over 25 ha
Peat Extraction	over 150 ha

Schedule 2

Quarries, Opencast and Peat Extraction

Underground Mining

Fluvial Dredging for Minerals

Deep Drillings

Surface Industrial Installations for extraction of coal, petroleum, natural gas, ores and bituminous shale (see also Section 4.4) over 0.5 ha

Other key legislation and guidance

Minerals Planning Guidance nos 3, 6, 7, 11
PPG 23 Planning and Pollution Control
EIA and Habitats (Extraction of Minerals by Marine Dredging) Regulations 2001
Groundwater Regulations 1998

Minerals Extraction

Potential issues/ EIA terms of reference	Potential impacts on the environment
Population	Public health Social effects on existing communities Nuisance
Transport	Nuisance Risk of pollution
Noise and vibration	Noise from blasting Noise from traffic
Ecology	Damage or loss to terrestrial or aquatic habitats
Land and soils	Subsidence Erosion or damage to soil Risk of pollution Effects on agriculture
Water	Hydrological disturbance to aquifers or watercourses Elevated suspended solids in watercourses Risk of pollution
Air and climate	Dust from blasting Dust and pollution from traffic
Cultural heritage	Loss or damage to historic features or their settings
Landscape	Visual impact and changes to landscape character
Use of resources	Waste management

Potential options for mitigation	Opportunities for environmental enhancement
Different mining technologies Alternative locations for infrastructure Environmental management Environmental liaison officer	New access and Rights of Way
Traffic management and timing Use of rail or water transport	New local road layouts Traffic calming
Timing of operations Acoustic barriers	–
Avoidance	Creation of new or additional habitats
Storage of topsoils Environmental management Access for agricultural users	Restoration to more appropriate land use
Environmental management	Restoration of watercourses
Timing of operations Damping down roads and vehicles	–
Avoidance Pre-development survey Watching brief	Education
Screening of operations, e.g. mounding and planting	New woodlands New hedgerows
Waste management plan	Recycling and reuse

Minerals Extraction

case example

Watts Blake Bearne (WBB), Devon

WBB have existing consents to extract ball clay for the manufacture of ceramic sanitary ware. This is a comparatively rare type of clay in the UK and the company was anxious to extend their workings across a lowland river in order to maximize extraction of the deposits and prolong the life of the workings. It was proposed to divert the river through agricultural land away from the deposits and photomontages were prepared to illustrate the effects and the mitigation proposed.

Photomontages are a useful way to illustrate predicted change. Here it was proposed to divert a river to permit mineral extraction.

Key fact

Preparation of an EMP and compliance through operations should be a requirement of any mineral development

Further information

Walsh, Lee and Wood, 1991
Environmental Assessment of Open Cast Coal Mines
EIA Centre, Manchester

Environment Agency, 1996 *Scoping Handbook*

CIRIA/Thomas Telford 1994
Environmental Assessment

British Geological Society

Sand and Gravel Association

Commitment to Restoration

Since restoration to an agreed standard is critical to the consenting of minerals extraction, regulatory bodies will require assurance of a commitment to such restoration. Some bodies frequently request payment of a bond prior to commencement of operations which is forfeited if restoration is not carried out (the bond can then be used by the regulator to undertake the restoration). If appropriate, phased restoration in the case of progressive quarrying or opencast mining can be implemented.

Restoration can include enhancement of the environment by planting of new woodlands (especially in advance of operations); improvement of watercourses; new hedgerows; new Rights of Way/access (including 'country park' type options for the local community); soil management; new roads and highways. Restoration may not always be to put back what was there before, e.g. agricultural land can be restored as lakes and wetlands: there can be opportunities for creative environmental design.

Before

After: On maturity

Monitoring

■ Archaeological watching brief during soil stripping.
■ Monitor for noise and dust in accordance with Environmental Health Officer (EHO) requirements.
■ Water quality of discharges and groundwater levels.
■ Compliance with agreed traffic management plan.
■ Compliance with:
  – predicted visual impact
  – ecological effects
  – land restoration
  – planting.

4.4 Energy

Characteristics of Energy Projects

- Safety and risk management essential.
- Includes fuel supply, production and transmission.
- Renewable energy projects offer sustainable development options.
- Non-renewable projects can affect climate change.
- Range of specific EIA Regulations under separate legislation.

Scope of EIA

Power stations need to be sited close to the source of energy (feedstock) and to cooling waters. They are, therefore, often sited in similar locations and potential cumulative impacts need to be addressed. In the case of waste to energy or combined heat and power plants, the energy source is likely to be principally domestic or commercial waste requiring the plant for economic reasons to be sited in or near urban areas, when air pollution and traffic will be a major concern.

For non-renewable projects, full Life Cycle Analysis is required. Fuel extraction, energy production and transmission processes with construction, operation and restoration phases for each should be addressed.

Windfarms frequently raise concerns of the effects on ecology, landscape and noise. In all instances, transmission lines result in visual impact as will overland pipelines.

The effects of the discharge of cooling water on the receiving aquatic environment have to be carefully considered and schemes designed to minimise any impacts.

Key Consultees

- Health and Safety Executive
- Local Authorities: planning, highways, environmental health
- Environment Agency
- National Radiological Protection Board
- Conservation, Heritage and community groups
- Countryside Agency
- English Nature
- English Heritage
- Department of Trade and Industry.

EIA Regulations Projects Schedule

Schedule 1

Crude oil refineries

Thermal power stations and other combustion installations over 500 t

Nuclear power stations

Nuclear fuel production, processing, reprocessing

Storage and disposal of radioactive waste

Extraction of petroleum and natural gas over 500 t/day, over 500,000 m^3/day (see also Section 4.3)

Pipelines for transport of gas, oil or chemicals over 800 mm diameter, over 40 km length

Storage of petroleum, petrochemical or chemical products over 200,000 t

Schedule 2

Production and transport of electricity, steam and hot water over 0.5/1.0 ha

Storage of gases and fossil fuels over 500 m^2 within 100 m of controlled waters

Industrial briquetting of coal and lignite over 1000 m^2

Processing and storage of radioactive waste over 1000 m^2 requires consent under RSA 1993

Hydroelectric energy production over 0.5 MW

Windfarms more than 2 turbines or hub height over 15 m

Key fact

The first EIA was for the Trans Alaska oil pipeline

Energy

Potential issues/ EIA terms of reference	Potential impacts on the environment
Population	Public health Risk of accidents Displacement (hydropower schemes)
Transport	Nuisance Risk of pollution
Noise and vibration	Construction noise especially drilling Low-frequency noise (windfarms) Noise from traffic Production and processing noise
Ecology	Temporary disturbance during construction (pipelines) Bird strike effects (windfarms) Intertidal communities (barrages)
Land and soils	Effects on agriculture (pipelines) Temporary topsoil storage
Water	Cooling water discharges Risk of pollution Effects on hydrology
Air and climate	Cumulative effects of emissions Climate change
Cultural heritage	Loss or damage to historic features or other settings
Landscape	Visual impact (especially windfarms)
Use of resources	Renewables can lead to positive effects Waste management, storage and treatment

Potential options for mitigation	Opportunities for environmental enhancement
Health and safety plan Pollution contingency plan Hazard, risk and environmental management	Recreation and amenity from hydropower and barrage schemes
Traffic management Use of rail or waterborne transport	New local road layouts Traffic calming
Timing of construction Acoustic barriers Avoidance of populated areas	–
Avoidance of habitats Adherence to agreed methods Creation of alternative habitats	Creation of new habitats
Maintenance of access for agricultural users	–
Environmental management Process design Water reuse	Restoration of watercourses
Use of renewable options contributes to climate change targets	–
Avoidance Pre-development survey Watching brief	–
Avoidance of sensitive areas Screening	New woodlands/hedgerows
Use of renewable options Waste management	Recycling and reuse

Energy

case example

Gas pipeline

A proposed gas pipeline had to cross a wetland of international importance. Whilst a route was selected to cross the wetland at the narrowest point, detailed studies were required to determine the impact of the crossing on the aquatic environment and associated fauna and flora. Working methods were specified and a commitment was made in the ES to ensure compliance.

Other key legislation and guidance

Nuclear Installations Act 1965

Pipelines Act 1975

Electricity Act 1989

Environmental Protection Act 1990

Water Resources Act 1991

Radioactive Substances Act 1993 (amended)

Large Combustion Plant (New Plant) Directive 1995

Groundwater Regulations 1998

Pollution Prevention and Control Act 1999 and Regulations 2000

PPG 22 Planning and Renewable Energy 1993

PPG 23 Planning and Pollution Control 1994 (under revision)

UK Climate Change Programme 2000

Nuclear Reactors (EIA for Decommissioning) Regulations 1999

Offshore Petroleum Production and Pipe-line (Assessment of Environmental Effects) Regulations 1999

Public Gas Transporter Pipe-line Works (EIA) Regulations 1999

Electricity Works (Assessment of Environmental Effects) Regulations 2000

Pipe-line Works (EIA) Regulations 2000

Further information

National Grid

National Radiological Protection Board

HSE

ETSU

Environment Agency National Groundwater and Contaminated Land Centre

British Wind Energy Association

Confederation of Renewable Energy Associations

COSHH A Brief Guide to the Regulations, 1999, HSE

Guidelines for the Environmental Assessment of Cross Country Pipelines, 1992, DTI

IPPC A Practical Guide, 2000, DETR

Pollution Handbook, 2000, NSCA

22nd Report Energy – The Changing Climate, 2000, RCEP

Environment Agency 1996 Scoping Handbook

Pipeline Industries Guild

Extract from ES demonstrating working methods of pipeline construction.

Commitment to Construction Techniques and Environmental Management Plans

It has long been recognized that long distance, below ground, pipelines can have potentially damaging effects if careful working methods are not followed. Apart from safety aspects and pollution risk in the event of fracture, pipelines can act as a drain and affect hydrological features; a barrier to wildlife and, if not properly restored, can be visually apparent and reduce habitat or agricultural land quality. For this reason, pipeline promoters made an early commitment to the principles of environmental management planning.

For each project, an EMP has to be produced to ensure that valued features are protected, working methods are employed and restoration to the required standard is carried out. It is customary to include an outline in the ES of these proposals so that they can be conditioned and monitored by the authorizing authority and so that contractors have an indication of environmental constraints.

Monitoring

- Routine discharges of radiation to the environment.
- Cooling water quantities and characteristics especially temperature and disinfectants.
- Noise and emissions to air.
- Restoration compliance.

4.5 Wastes Management

Characteristics of Wastes Management Projects

■ Only some 25% of wastes generated in the UK is controlled waste – the rest comes from agriculture (20%) and mining/quarrying/demolition.

■ Waste management is based on the hierarchy of reduce, reuse, recycle.

■ A key feature is energy recovery or production of compost from waste.

■ For 'temporary' projects such as landfill or landraising, a commitment to restoration is important and can result in enhancement, especially of mineral workings.

Scope of EIA

The range of methods of waste management leads to very different effects. Landfill or landraising, usually based on a completed mineral project, will entail a continuation of the same type of activities in terms of movement of plant and materials. New hazards may arise such as landfill gas, leachate, odour and noise – visual impact is frequently an important issue. The EIA has also to consider the length of time the scheme will last and the restoration proposals and commitments.

Other waste management facilities such as incineration, chemical treatment, waste transfer or recycling stations require built development, plant and possibly exhaust stacks. Incinerators may emit harmful gases and chemicals from incomplete combustion. In all instances though traffic noise and movement is likely to be a key issue.

Proposed landfill sites based on worked out and abandoned mineral sites have to pay particular attention to ecological issues since such sites are frequently colonized by rare or protected species; bats in particular favour caves or fissures in mineral workings.

The location of sites for storage or disposal of wastes is always contentious due to the public perception of nuisance and health risk.

Key Consultees

■ Health and Safety Executive

■ Environment Agency

■ Local Authorities: planning, waste, highways, environmental health, conservation

■ Countryside Agency

■ English Nature

■ English Heritage

■ Conservation, Heritage and community groups.

The UK Waste Strategy 2000 is based on four principles:
■ Best practicable environmental option
■ Regional self-sufficiency
■ Proximity principle
■ Waste hierarchy

EIA Regulations Projects Schedule

Schedule 1

Incineration, chemical treatment, landfill of hazardous waste

Incineration, chemical treatment of non-hazardous waste exceeding 100 t/day

Schedule 2

Installations for the disposal of waste not included in Schedule 1

Sludge deposition sites

Key fact

The Duty of Care is a statutory requirement that all producers or keepers of waste must prevent it causing pollution or harm

Key fact

In 1999, the UK recovered 9% of its waste (the lowest in the EU) compared to the best, Germany with 40%

– Resource Recovery Forum 2000

Other key legislation and guidance

Environmental Protection Act 1990

Environment Act 1995

Radioactive Substances Act 1993

Waste Management Licensing Regulations 1994

Controlled and Special Waste Regulations 1996

Landfill Tax Regulations 1996

PPC Regulations 2000

PPG 10 Planning and Waste Management 1999

PPG 23 Planning and Pollution Control

DETR 2000 UK Waste Strategy

Wastes Management

Potential issues/EIA terms of reference	Potential impacts on the environment
Population	Perceived and actual public health risks Nuisance (vermin, litter, etc.)
Transport	Traffic generated during construction, operation and restoration
Noise and vibration	Increased noise levels during construction Traffic noise including reversing alarms
Ecology	Loss of habitat and protected species from restoration of minerals workings
Land and soils	Land contamination Temporary loss of agricultural land
Water	Leachate from landfill – pollution of surface or groundwaters
Air and climate	Landfill gas Odour (perceived or actual) Dust and particulates Pollutants from incomplete combustion
Cultural heritage	Loss of heritage features
Landscape	Change or loss of valued landscape Visual impact (e.g. stack or landraising)
Use of resources	Loss of potential resources Waste management, storage and treatment

Potential options for mitigation	Opportunities for environmental enhancement
Good operational management Community liaison Site design and facilities	Restoration of derelict land Recreational and amenity afteruse
Traffic management plans Designated haul routes	–
Good operational management Acoustic screens and housings	–
Avoid sites of ecological interest Relocation as a last resort	Restoration to more varied habitat and biodiversity
Soils storage, handling and management	Composting for soil restoration Restoration of derelict land to appropriate use
Landfill design Leachate collection and treatment	Restoration of watercourses
Good operational management Site design Gas scrubbing Negative pressure at sources of emissions	Waste to energy
Avoid sites of heritage interest Archaeological watching brief	–
Screening Site design Planting	Restoration of degraded landscape
Waste minimization Recycling and reuse Domestic waste separation	Composting Waste to energy

Wastes Management

Further information

NSCA Pollution Handbook 2000

www.environment-agency.gov.uk

DETR 2000 IPPC: A Practical Guide

Chartered Institute of Wastes Management
(CInstWM)

Environment Agency 1996 Scoping Handbook

Cumulative Impacts

The EU Landfill directive is reducing the quantity of waste that can be taken to landfill. Also, the remaining capacity of landfill sites in the UK is limited. Therefore, there is increasing pressure to seek other methods of waste treatment and management. This is likely to increase the need for incineration which has the added bonus of utilizing the heat from waste combustion for energy generation. However, incinerators can emit toxins such as dioxins and heavy metals giving the technique a poor public image. If the waste management industry pursues the incineration option, it will be necessary to consider the **cumulative impacts** of these plants, especially in the more populated areas.

Monitoring

- Archaeological watching brief.
- Monitor for noise and dust in accordance with EHO requirements.
- Water quality of leachate, surface water and groundwater.
- Compliance with agreed traffic management plan.
- Compliance with predicted: visual impact, ecology, land restoration, planting.
- Stack emissions in accordance with Pollution Prevention and Control (PPC) requirements.

case example

Landfill ES

A landraising operation in greenbelt on the edge of a major conurbation had been operated successfully for many years with landfill gas management and leachate treatment. Access was good and, being near to the city, this contributed to the satisfactory operation of the site. It was proposed to extend the scheme and provide a Materials Recycling Facility (MRF). The mitigation proposed was to plant extensive woodland to link with a new urban forest together with restoration of a channelized watercourse. An agreement was entered into to manage the woodland for a 100 years for the benefit of the local community as a Country Park – demonstrating the commitment to mitigation.

Restored landfill

4.6 Water

Characteristics of Water Projects

- Includes dams, reservoirs, water mains and pipelines, treatment works, coast and river flood protection.
- See also Section 4.4 – Hydroelectric and barrage schemes.
- Incorporation of Sustainable Urban Drainage systems (SUDS), where appropriate, into other development types.
- New and improved infrastructure can provide major environmental and social benefits.
- In UK planning – issues with water companies, regulators (EA and Ofwat) and LPAs.
- Compliance with other directives is often required; wastewater schemes shall also consider the effects of sludge production.

Scope of EIA

Of particular interest in water schemes is careful consideration of alternatives. This can range from decisions on whether to defend a coastline to demand management to avoid the need for a reservoir. Development of reservoirs in particular can involve the enforced resettlement of communities and the loss of cultural heritage assets: this can provoke strong opposition and the principles promoted by the World Commission on Dams (2000) can avoid confrontation. The cumulative impacts, which can have transfrontier effects, are important to address.

New sewerage or sewage/wastewater treatment schemes in previously unsewered or overloaded systems in urban environments can create substantial temporary disturbance. The siting of treatment plants will often be contentious, primarily due to the perception of nuisance (odour and noise) – despite their evident benefits.

The provision of coastal defences frequently leads to competing views between landowners and conservationists. In all cases, thorough consultation is essential.

Key Consultees

- Local Authorities: planning, environmental health, conservation, highways
- Environment Agency
- Port Health Authorities
- Sea Fisheries Committees
- Conservation, Heritage and community groups
- Countryside Agency
- DEFRA
- English Nature
- English Heritage.

EIA Regulations Projects Schedule

Schedule 1

Groundwater abstraction or recharge where volume is 10 million m³/year or more

Water transfer schemes between river basins

Wastewater treatment plants with capacity exceeding 150,000 population equivalent

Dams where water stored exceeds 10 million m³

Schedule 2

Groundwater abstraction, water transfer, wastewater treatment plants and dams not included in Schedule 1

Canalization and flood relief works exceeding 1 ha

case example

Wastewater treatment plants have been built under carparks or underground without causing nuisance to local residents.

Key fact

Water needs to be considered within the context of strategic planning such as catchment management planning

Key fact

The Environment Agency will not give land drainage consent to development proposals which include culverting of surface water

Water

Potential issues/EIA terms of reference	Potential impacts on the environment
Population	Social effects on existing communities Public health Actual effect often beneficial Nuisance
Transport	Traffic during construction New haul routes
Noise and vibration	Noise from construction Noise from operation – plant and activities
Ecology	Damage or loss of habitat and biodiversity
Land and soils	Effects on agriculture Contamination
Water	Temporary discharges/risk of pollution during construction Hydrology – loss of flow Pollution incidents and run-off
Air and climate	Odour (perceived or actual) Dust and particulates during construction
Cultural heritage	Loss of buildings, features or settings
Landscape	Visual impacts of dams, treatment works, coastal defences Temporary effects of pipelines
Use of resources	Loss of water resource

Potential options for mitigation	Opportunities for environmental enhancement
Backstop dams to protect communities Relocation and resettlement	Recreation and amenity on new lakes and restored rivers Improved bathing waters Improved shell fisheries
Traffic management plans Haul routes below proposed water level	–
Acoustic screens/housings Quiet machinery and plant	–
Avoidance of valued areas Backstop dams to protect features Translocation	Improved/additional ecological features River restoration
–	–
Containment measures Provision of compensation water SUDS	Use of SUDS River restoration Improved fisheries Improved water quality
Odour control measures Alternative technologies	–
Backstop dams to protect features Archaeological watching brief	–
Design dams to integrate into setting Reduce scale of plant Screening, mounding Avoidance of sensitive locations	Additional woodland River restoration
Recycling and reuse SUDS Energy efficient plant Waste to Energy	Sustainable water management Provision of treated sewage sludge for soil conditioning Potential for hydropower

Water

case example

Technologies for water treatment are such that imaginative design solutions can be used for locations in small, urban and sensitive areas

Other key legislation and guidance

Water Resources Act 1991

Water Industries Act 1991

Land Drainage Act 1991

Environmental Protection Act 1995

Habitats Regulations 1994

Urban Waste Water Treatment Directive (UWWTD)

Bathing Waters Directive

Shellfish Hygiene Directive

Shellfish Waters Directive

Freshwater Fish Directive

Wild Birds Directive

Water Framework Directive 2001

PPG 23 Planning and Pollution Control

PPG 25 Development and Flood Risks 2001

Further information

Local Environment Agency Plans (LEAPs)

Coastal and Shoreline Management Plans (CMPs and SMPs)

Environment Agency 1996 Scoping Handbook

Water Companies

RSPB

Chartered Institution of Water and Environmental Management (CIWEM)

Centre for Ecology and Hydrology (CEH)

Sustainable Urban Drainage Systems (SUDS)

Development alters the existing state of drainage in an area with impermeable surfaces such as roads/roofs directing surface water from a site which can result in local flooding and pollution. The sustainable management of surface and groundwater regimes has a role to play in the achievement of sustainable development. Sustainable drainage is the practice of controlling surface water run-off as close to its origin as possible before discharging into a watercourse or the ground.

There are a wide range of sustainable drainage options available and the Environment Agency can advise on the most suitable application depending on the characteristics of the receiving environment. Examples include: rainwater recycling; filterstrips and swales; filter drains and permeable porous surfaces; infiltration; basins and ponds.

Sustainable drainage has many benefits relating to a variety of environmental issues such as reducing flood risk, minimizing diffuse pollution from run-off, reducing pollution to aquifers, minimizing erosion and damage to habitats, maintaining or restoring natural flow regimes to receiving watercourses, and maintaining groundwater recharge.

Monitoring

- Consented Discharges
- Licensed Abstraction
- Bathing Water
- Odour/noise
- Compensation flows.

River Restoration (during contruction and then after). Many local drainage and flood alleviation schemes in the 1950s–1970s resulted in the straightening or culverting of rivers. New works associated with rivers should consider the restoration of rivers to their original courses which also provides for enhanced assimilative capacity of pollution loads by the provision of reed beds, meanders and off-line ponds.

4.7 Housing and Mixed Use Development

Characteristics of Housing and Mixed Use Projects

- Government seeks to reduce dependence on the car by planning for mixed use.
- Mixed use includes residential, commercial and recreational.
- Housing demands are increasing due to demography and requirement for single-occupancy accommodation. Therefore, housing may be the greatest potential cause of environmental impact from new development.
- Requirement to meet social housing targets.
- The key characteristics are associated with transport.

Key fact

'Housing' as such is not mentioned in the EIA Regulations but is taken to be included within 'urban development projects'

LPAs should .... *'give priority to re-using previously-developed land within urban areas ... in preference to the development of greenfield sites'*
– PPG 3 2000

Scope of EIA

The scope is dependent on location: if rural and under development pressure, issues focus on loss of greenspace; in urban areas, issues are about regeneration and increased density; whilst on the urban fringe, issues can be about integration and access.

The local plan will identify land use and relevant environmental issues. Government requirements to use brownfield rather than greenfield can cause conflict with sustainability issues for accessibility and ecology. Derelict and contaminated sites can be isolated from good transport links and may be of greater ecological value due to lack of disturbance than greenfield sites, which themselves have suffered from intensive agriculture.

All stages of development – site preparation, construction and occupation – need to be considered, and design should be led by sustainable principles (e.g. BREEAM standards). Early consideration of a community/residents' management plan is useful, especially when habitats or flood risk management (SUDS) measures are required.

Key Consultees

- Local authorities: planning, waste, highways, environmental health, conservation
- Environment Agency
- Department for Environment, Food and Rural Affairs; Department of Transport, Local Government and the Regions
- Utility companies
- Development Agencies
- Chambers of Commerce
- Commission for Architecture and the Built Environment
- English Nature
- English Heritage
- Countryside Agency
- Conservation, heritage and community groups.

EIA Regulations Projects Schedule

Schedule 1

Schedule 2

Infrastructure projects if development area exceeds 0.5 ha

- Industrial estates
- Urban development projects, including the construction of shopping centres and carparks, sports stadiums, leisure centres and multiplex cinemas

Housing and Mixed Use Development

Potential issues/EIA terms of reference	Potential impacts on the environment
Population	Integration with existing communities (domination/balance) Disturbance and loss of amenity Domination of competing settlements/neighbourhoods
Transport	Increased traffic generation leads to congestion – highway capacity Provision of new transport links/nodes/systems Increased risk of accidents; increased car parks
Noise and vibration	Noise levels from traffic, site clearance, demolition and construction, e.g. piling – can affect both humans and wildlife Affect on listed buildings from vibration
Ecology	Loss and fragmentation of habitats and disturbance to species Severance of wildlife corridors
Land and soils	Loss of geological SSSI exposures Disturbance of contaminated land Loss of best agricultural land
Water	Surface water run off; effects on groundwater and river flows Pollution from storage and accidents Water supply, sewerage and sewage treatment provision Floodplain and coastal encroachment
Air and climate	Effects of dust and emissions on population and sensitive habitats and species, buildings and structures Contribution to climate change
Cultural heritage	Loss or damage to historic feature, landscape or building Loss or degradation of local identity
Landscape	Creation of visual impact and loss of valued landscape character
Use of resources	Loss and consumption of natural resources Contribution to climate change Production of waste

Potential options for mitigation	Opportunities for environmental enhancement
Community input into design development and requirements for provision of facilities	Improved recreation/leisure facilities Public open space Improved transport links and facilities
Traffic calming; traffic routing Restrict private car use/ownership Contribution to public transport provision	Physical fitness Highway improvements – cycle/walkways Car-free areas
Timing of activities; traffic routing Quiet equipment/machinery Acoustic barriers; double glazing	Reduction of existing noise levels by alternative traffic routings and insulation
Avoiding sensitive areas whether designated or not Phasing construction to avoid breeding or migration Relocation of species, translocation of habitats Creation of new habitats	Improvement to biodiversity integrated within provision of open space or buildings Community involvement in ecological management
Site and development design to avoid or treat contaminated land Recreation of geological exposures	Enhance exposures Decontamination of brownfield sites
SUDS Grey water recycling Flood storage area provision Pollution control measures via EMP	Restoration of degraded rivers and natural functioning of floodplains Habitat creation; provision of amenity Sewage treatment for unsewered areas
BREEAM design standards Site selection and orientation of buildings Construction methods and site control	Reduction in energy demand contributing to climate change targets
Avoidance Pre-development investigations On site monitoring and watching brief	Restoration or improvement of setting
Site selection Building or structure heights and design Landscape creation – planting, bund Colour and material selection	Improvement of setting Creation of new woodlands Public open space provision
Use of recycled materials for construction waste minimisation, recycling and reuse	–

Housing and Mixed Use Development

Case example

New Settlement south of the M4

Wokingham District Council was required to make an allocation in the emerging local plan for a new settlement of up to 5000 houses. Three alternative sites were promoted by potential developers for inclusion in the plan. Each proposal was accompanied by an ES and the District Council sought to ensure that the ESs were of equal quality so that the sites could be compared by the Inspector on their merits rather than be jeopardized by inadequacies in the ES

"

Achieving an urban renaissance is .... about creating the quality of life and vitality that makes urban living so desirable. We must bring about a change in urban attitudes

– Urban Task Force 1999   "

Other key legislation and guidance

Local Government Act 2000

PPG 3 Housing

PPG 7 The Countryside

PPG 13 Transport

PPG 23 Planning and Pollution Control

PPG 25 Development and Flood Risks

DETR 2000 Urban and Rural White Papers

Urban Task Force 1999 Towards an Urban Renaissance

DETR 1999 The New Deal for Communities

Further information

Barton *et al*. 2002 Shaping Neighbourhoods

Building Research Establishment Environmental Assessment Methods (BREEAM)

DETR 2000 Sustainable Construction

Environment Agency 1996 Scoping Handbook

House Builders Federation (HBF)

Town & Country Planning Association (TCPA)

Royal Town Planning Institute (RTPI)

DETR Home Energy Efficiency

Green roof for habitat and water management   *Photo courtesy of Alumasc*

Promotion of Sustainable Development: Key Features

- Energy efficient construction and buildings.
- Sustainable transport including Local Transport Plans and Travel Plans.
- Waste minimization, recycling and reuse.
- Local Combined Heat and Power.
- Avoidance of floodplains or provision of compensation flood storage.
- Sustainable Urban Drainage Systems.
- Grey water recycling, where appropriate.
- Provision of open space.
- Enhancing biodiversity, maintenance of ecological networks, creation of habitats.
- Environmental Management Plans (construction and occupation).

Monitoring

- Community Management Plans
- Monitoring for noise and dust in accordance with EHO requirements
- Traffic Management Plan compliance
- Flood storage facilities and SUDS management.

4.8 Transport

Characteristics of Transport Projects

- Often linear (roads, railways and canals) and long distance.
- Can apply to on-line widening of existing routes or development of new routes.
- New routes are often highly contentious leading to polarization of public opinion.
- Locally, new roads can create air and noise pollution and severance; globally, traffic contributes to climate change.
- Bypasses can resolve congestion in towns and villages but can also lead to their isolation.
- Traffic effects are associated with most types of development.

Scope of EIA

The scope of EIA studies associated with roads and bridges is clearly set out in the Design Manual for Roads and Bridges Volume 11.

Specific methods have been developed for Traffic Impact Assessment (TIA). However, the scope of a TIA is different from that required for the ES and close liaison between the traffic, air and noise consultants is especially important. These assessments have to take into account future use of the routes, i.e. the level of traffic and emissions in the 'baseline/opening year' and a 'future year'.

Surface water run-off from roads has implications for receiving watercourses; water quality and hydrological assessments are required, together with construction of flood storage and pollution control processes. Existing roads and railways are often havens for wildlife given the relatively undisturbed nature of verges and sidings; derelict railway sidings in particular can have developed valued habitat for rare or unusual species. Consideration has to be given to both vertical and horizontal alignments when developing a new transport corridor – this can have particular effects on visibility. Acoustic bunds can also have unacceptable visual impacts.

The scope of the EIA should also include factors of physical fitness (encouraging cycling and walking) and journey ambience (traveller stress and views) in accordance with government policy ('A New Deal for Transport').

Key Consultees

- Local Authorities: planning, highways, conservation, environmental health
- Civil Aviation Authority
- Port and Harbour Authorities
- Navigation Authorities
- Public transport operators
- Ramblers Association
- Boat Owners Association
- Conservation, heritage and community groups
- DTLR
- DEFRA
- British Waterways
- Railtrack
- English Nature
- English Heritage
- Sustrans
- Highways Agency
- Countryside Agency
- Living Streets

Key fact

One of the longest public inquiries in UK planning history was associated with Terminal 5 at Heathrow Airport

Key fact

Although legislation has had a significant effect at reducing the pollution from vehicles, this will be balanced by the predicted increase in traffic

EIA Regulations Projects Schedule

Schedule 1

Railways and Airports (runway length 2100 m or more)

Motorways and express roads (EU traffic artery)

Inland Waterways and Ports (vessels over 1350 t)

Trading Ports and piers (vessels over 1350 t)

Schedule 2

Railways and international transhipment facilities and terminals (not in Schedule 1)

Airfields (not in Schedule 1)

Roads, harbours and port installations (not in Schedule 1)

Inland waterways, canalization and flood-relief works

Tramways, elevated and underground railways

Transport

Potential issues/EIA terms of reference	Potential impacts on the environment
Population	Severance and isolation Loss or degradation of amenity Public health Risk of accidents
Transport	Delays during construction
Noise and vibration	Piling, tunnelling, blasting Vehicle movement
Ecology	Habitat loss, fragmentation or damage Disturbance Loss or damage to wildlife corridors
Land and soils	Landtake Sterilization of minerals Damage or contamination
Water	Contamination from run-off Effects on groundwater or surface water flows and levels
Air and climate	Dust and particulates Gaseous emissions – global/climate change – local air quality
Cultural heritage	Damage to listed buildings from vibration Land settlement Effect on setting and amenity of listed building and features
Landscape	Effect on character of valued or historic landscape Removal of features Restriction to views – visual intrusion Opening of views
Use of resources	Demand for construction materials

Potential options for mitigation mitigation	Opportunities for environmental enhancement
Change of alignment Footbridges and underpasses	Improved amenity, tranquility and accessibility Physical fitness Safety improvements
Adherence to Traffic Management Plan Travel Plans for occupiers Timing to avoid holiday periods Traffic calming	Improved journey times
Noise insulation Construction methods Change of alignment Screening	Improved quality of life for bypassed villages and towns
Change of alignment Protection of valued areas and features Timing of construction Maintaining ecological networks Tunnels for, e.g. badgers, deer	Creation of new habitats Restoration of watercourses SUDS
Alignment to minimize landtake Negotiation for land exchange Extract minerals prior to construction Soils storage and handling EMP	–
SUDS EMP	Ecological and amenity value from SUDS
EMP Wheelwashing, sheeting of lorries	Improved emissions quality from reduced congestion Electric vehicles, trains, trams (depending on power source)
Change of alignment Preservation *in situ* Excavation and recording Archaeological watching brief	–
Change of alignment Screening – mounding and planting Quality of design	Improved traveller views
Reuse of materials Energy efficiency during construction	Fuel saving by improved routes

case example

On appeal for an outline application for a business park it was ruled that, in accordance with PPG 13 Transport, an unacceptable development could not be approved just because a Green Transport Plan was proposed. In this instance the site was relatively inaccessible by public transport and remote from settlements so walking and cycling were not realistic options; private cars would remain the main form of transport. While the applicants proposed a Green Transport Plan in the ES, there was clearly concern about how effective this would be

Other key legislation and guidance

DETR 2001 Transport 2010: The 10 Year Plan

DETR 1998 Transport White Paper – A New Deal for Transport

Transport Act 2000

Transport and Works Act 1992

PPG 13 Transport

RCEP 1997 20th Report Transport and the Environment

DETR 1999 Sustainable Distribution Strategy

DETR 2000 Road Safety Strategy

DETR 2000 Guidance on the Methodology for Multi-Modal Studies (GOMMMS)

DETR 1999 Places, Streets and Movement

DETR 2000 A Good Practice Guide for the Development of Local Transport Plans

IEA 1993 Guidelines for the Environmental Assessment of Road Traffic

IHT 1994 Guidelines for Traffic Impact Assessment

HA 1993 Design Manual for Roads and Bridges Vol 11: Environmental Assessment

Further information

The Institution of Highways and Transportation

Inland Waterways Association

Transport Research Laboratory

Transport 2000

Sustrans

1996, Scoping Handbook Environment Agency

A New Approach to Appraisal (NATA)

The requirement for integrated transport has led to new appraisal methods for new roads and motorways in response to government policy (A New Deal for Transport 1998). Guidance on the Methodology for Multi-Modal Studies (GOMMMS) state that the appraisal should consider the objectives of: environment, safety, economy, accessibility and integration. This should be supported by other analyses: distribution and equity; affordability and financial sustainability; practicality and public acceptability. For environmental issues the technical guidelines contained within DMRB Volume 11 are followed in stages using a multi-modal study approach, e.g.

Stage 1: assess options – road or rail?
Stage 2: assess routes.
Stage 3: assess impacts.

For each stage GOMMMS requires worksheets to be completed with the results embracing all objectives presented in Appraisal Summary Tables (ASTs).

Travel Plans and Local Transport Plans

A Travel Plan (formerly a Green Transport Plan) is a package of initiatives for employers to tackle different aspects of transport, including commuter journeys, business travel and fleet management.

Local Transport Plans (LTPs) are for local authorities to help better integrate transport policy and embrace the full range of transport issues.

Monitoring

- Archaeological watching brief
- Noise, dust and air quality during construction as in EMP
- Water discharges and receiving waters
- Compliance with agreed Traffic Management Plan
- Compliance with predicted impacts, e.g. visual impact
- Compliance with requirements, e.g. planting.

Chapter 5

Environmental Management

Contents

5.1   Introduction

5.2   Definitions

5.3   Discussion

5.4   Methodology

Environmental management reduces the risk of pollution to the environment and improves the sustainable management of environmental resources. This chapter introduces the role of environmental management in Environmental Impact Assessment and explains how commitments to mitigation and environmental protection can be made in a systematic and transparent way.

5.1   Introduction

This chapter describes the relationship between EIA and Environmental Management during construction, operation/occupation and restoration – which is generally controlled via an Environmental Management Plan (EMP). The EMP has links to Environmental Management Systems (EMSs) which are more usually adopted for industrial activities/processes and their organizational procedures, since both are aimed at the management of environmental risk. EMSs may be independently audited against a formally accredited system such as EMAS or ISO14001. The maintenance of an EMS by the developer, operator and/or contractor facilitates the environmental management of site preparation, construction and later activities since appropriate procedures are already in place and are part of the organization's policies, protocols and culture. The inclusion of an EMP or EMS will provide additional reassurance to the regulators and the public.

Further information

ISO14001: Environmental Management Systems

EMAS European Eco-Management and Audit Scheme

www.bsi-global.com

www.ciria.org.uk

5.2   Definitions

Since environmental management in relation to EIA is a relatively recent concept, a number of terms are being used by different institutions and organizations. These are some of those in most common use:

- EMP (Environmental Management Plan): Generic term and refers to the construction period but can also more generally refer to arrangements for environmental management during occupation/operation as well.
- CEMP (Construction (or Contract) Environmental Management Plan): To be prepared by or for contractors before they commence on a development site; often part of contract documentation.
- SEMP (Site Environmental Management Plan): Prepared by site owners or operators for long-term environmental maintenance and management of the site.
- HEMP (Handover Environmental Management Plan): For Design and Build contracts. Prepared by the contractor on completion of construction for future environmental maintenance and management.
- WMP (Waste Management Plan): Specifically based on the requirements of the Environmental Protection Act 1990. Identifies types of wastes arisings, their management, documentation and treatment/disposal.

An ES EMP provides:

- Checklist for regulators
- Commitments to mitigation
- Starting point for tender specification

A Contract EMP provides:

- Communication systems
- Environmental policy statements
- Method statements
- CVs and training
- Auditing and monitoring

■ TMP (Traffic Management Plan): Identifies safe and agreed routings of traffic during construction and operation. Includes any restrictions on timing of access.

5.3 Discussion

There is no requirement or reference to the need for auditing or monitoring of site activities to be mentioned in the ES. However, it has been standard practice for some years, particularly in the oil and gas industry, to require an EMP before site work is commenced. This has led to various practitioners and commentators to recognize the usefulness of providing in the ES an indication of how the construction and operational activities will be managed insofar as they may potentially affect the environment.

The EMP is developed and designed through consultation between the design team, regulators and competent authorities, and the local community. It achieves the following objectives:

■ to identify predictions, activities and commitments in the ES which may require specific conditions/agreements, consents or licences from the competent authorities

■ to ensure that contract documentation and detailed design addresses the relevant mitigation measures agreed during the EIA process and that the contractors allow for this in the tendering process. In this respect the EMP should be prescriptive yet flexible enough to allow for innovation

■ to provide specific Method Statements for procedures when working near sensitive areas

■ to ensure that the developers/operators are clear about the mitigation commitments and means of their implementation

■ to ensure that systems are in place to resolve any potential problems associated with the site activities

■ to comply with relevant legislation, standards and guidance.

This approach is becoming more relevant now that many contracts are procured via the Design and Build process. This requires the contractor's team to take responsibility for the preparation of the ES and the EMP in parallel, thus ensuring integration of environmental risk minimization into the design and build activities. It may also be linked, for example to Considerate Constructors Schemes which have been adopted as codes of practice in some cities.

Considerate Constructors Scheme:

■ Considerate

■ Environment

■ Cleanliness

■ Good neighbour

■ Accountable

■ Respectful

■ Responsible

■ Safe

EMPs have tended to focus on pollution prevention and control and the protection of the natural environment. However, they may also be used to promote sustainable use of resources including energy and construction materials. The EMP, therefore, has the added function of not only incorporating the mitigation of those environmental issues identified here in Chapter 3, but also encompasses other issues which may be raised during consultation. These can be of particular local concern, e.g. waste and litter, vermin and pests, sustainable construction, and wider global issues of energy use. The ES can, therefore, make a commitment to sustainability principles and progress towards sustainable development objectives.

5.4 Methodology

This section provides a model outline of the contents of the various EMPs. This outline can be used as a checklist in an ES to ensure that commitments are made and methods of implementation are identified. All sites, development types and contracts differ to a degree so it can be adapted to suit the particular circumstances.

CEMP

Consultation and Liaison Arrangements

The EIA process will have covered considerable consultation with local residents and other interested parties as well as the regulatory authorities. This section describes how this is to be maintained through the duration of the project. The construction team may set up a local Environmental Liaison Group to advise and monitor environmental concerns during construction activities and programming. This is particularly important to advise local businesses or residents of any particularly disturbing activities, e.g. noise, traffic movements. It also provides details of contacts in the event of any complaints and procedures for responding.

Method Statements

These include all the measures agreed during the EIA with the regulatory authorities. They may address the following activities:

- soil handling, storage and reinstatement
- reinstatement of habitats
- waste management plan
- noise prevention and abatement
- protection of existing habitats and species
- implementation of new planting and seeding
- landscape and ecology management plan
- use of herbicides
- public rights of way
- pollution control and contingency procedures
- construction compounds, haul routes, borrow pits, lay down areas and batching plants
- archaeological management
- drainage features
- working times
- traffic management plan
- energy and other resources use.

Specific contents of some of the above include:

Waste Management Plan. This identifies types of wastes arising from the works activities together with the appropriate segregation, storage, handling, transfer and disposal procedures. Documentation and record keeping for the identification, transfer of wastes and final treatment/disposal are required in accordance with Waste Management – A Duty of Care (DoE 1991).

Contents of a CEMP:

1. Consultation and liaison arrangements
2. Method statements
3. Environmental policy
4. CVs of environmental personnel
5. Training
6. Auditing and monitoring

Key fact

Appointing a project Environmental Liaison officer can help resolve any problems with the local community

---

Pollution Control and Contingency Plan. This identifies sensitive or vulnerable receptors and natural features, e.g. watercourses, and working methods to minimize environmental risk. It includes detailed procedures for the storage and use of materials, fuels, lubricants and any other environmentally hazardous substances and incident notification procedures for regulators. Requirements for pollution control equipment and protection measures for sensitive areas are identified.

Traffic Management Plan. This details the agreed and approved routes for each stage of the construction to minimize disturbance and to ensure that public highways are maintained in a safe condition. This, therefore, ensures road safety (e.g. avoidance of school access), road cleanliness (removal of mud from road), and minimal traffic disruption.

Archaeological Management. This includes arrangements for any advance works, archaeological watching briefs, protection of archaeological features, phasing of archaeological activities and archaeological recording.

Environmental Policy

This records the environmental policies of the contractor/developer and any certification under an accredited EMS, e.g. EMAS, ISO14001, and compliance with industry codes of practice. This demonstrates that the relevant organizations are committed to the highest standards of environmental performance and compliance with legislative requirements.

CVs of Environmental Personnel

These are provided (at tender stage if relevant initially) to ensure that such staff have relevant knowledge, experience and authority to monitor, audit and rectify any environmental issue. Personnel will include the Site Environmental Liaison Officer, environmental co-ordinators, specialists and other advisors.

Training

Site personnel, appropriate design staff and relevant visitors should receive induction training in accordance with the EMP; a record of competence and training given is maintained in the EMP. This will particularly apply to any sub-contractors.

Auditing and Monitoring

An Audit Plan should be prepared which details:

- how the site activities are monitored
- the frequency of such audits and checks
- who undertakes them and responsibilities
- reporting and actioning procedures.

SEMP/HEMP

These provide for the longer-term maintenance and management relating to environmental issues of the site. They describe the strategies for maintenance of all environmental areas and record how these will be achieved together with appropriate timetables and programmes. Such management can be undertaken by a range of organizations, but is often contracted to specialist companies. Of particular concern is to involve residents or occupiers in the formulation and implementation of these plans. Such plans include (but are not limited to):

- monitoring and maintenance of new planting
- management of existing hedgerows and woodlands
- maintenance of pollution control systems including oil interceptors
- maintenance of domestic sewage treatment plants
- maintenance of public open space and footpaths
- maintenance of sustainable drainage systems especially flood alleviation ponds
- monitoring (e.g. water quality, species, habitats, noise, air quality)
- energy and water resource use
- waste management.

Key features of Environmental Management

- An EMS gives confidences to regulators and the community
- Environmental Management reduces risk of pollution and improves sustainable management of resources
- provides commitment to implementation of mitigation in the ES
- EMPs are relevant for a variety of developer/contractor/regulator relationships.

Protection of environmental resource during construction   Photo by AC Archaeology

Appendices

1. Further Guidance

2. Schedule 2 Projects: Thresholds and Criteria

3. Schedule 4: Content of Environmental Statements

4. Review Criteria

5. Bibliography and References

6. Organizations

7. Training Courses

Appendix 1

Further Guidance: Key Consultees and Sources of Information

Name:	Botanical Society for the British Isles (BSBI)
Tel.:	01283 568136 (Hon. Gen. Sec.)
Website:	http://www.BSBI.org.uk

Name:	British Trust for Ornithology (BTO)
Tel.:	01842 750050
Address:	BTO, The Nunnery, Thetford, Norfolk, IP24 2PU
Website:	http://www.bto.org/

Name:	British Waterways
Tel.:	01923 201120
Address:	Customer Services, British Waterways, Willow Grange, Church Road, Watford, WD17 4QA
Website:	http://www.britishwaterways.org.uk/

Name:	Construction Industry Research and Information Association (CIRIA)
Tel.:	020 7222 8891
Address:	6 Storey's Gate, London SW1P 3AU
Website:	http://www.ciria.org.uk/

Name:	Countryside Council for Wales (CCW)
Tel.:	01248 385500
Address:	Headquarters CCW, Plas Penrhos, Ffordd Penrhos, Bangor, Gwynedd, LL57 2LQ
Website:	http://www.ccw.gov.uk/

Name:	Centre for Ecology and Hydrology (CEH)
Tel.:	01491 838800
Address:	Maclean Building, Crowmarsh Gifford, Wallingford, Oxon OX10 8BB
Website:	http://www.ceh-nerc.ac.uk

Name:	Countryside Agency
Tel.:	01242 521381
Address:	John Dower House, Crescent Place, Cheltenham, Gloucestershire, GL50 3RA
Website:	http://www.countryside.gov.uk/

Name:	Council for the Protection of Rural England (CPRE)
Tel.:	020 7976 6433
Address:	CPRE, Warwick House, 25 Buckingham Palace Road, London, SW1W 0PP
Website:	http://www.cpre.org.uk/

Name:	Department of Agriculture and Rural Development, Northern Ireland
Tel.:	028 9052 4999
Address:	Dundonald House, Upper Newtownards Road, Belfast, BT4 3SB
Website:	http://www.dardni.gov.uk/

Name: Department of Environment, Northern Ireland
Tel.:   028 9054 0540
Address: Clarence Court, 10–18 Adelaide Street, Belfast, BT1 2GB
Website: http://www.nics.gov.uk/env.htm

Name: Department of Environment, Northern Ireland – Planning Service
Tel.:   028 9054 0540
Address: Headquarters, Clarence Court, Adelaide Street, Belfast, BT2 8GB
Website: http://www.doeni.gov.uk/planning/index.htm

Name: Department for Environment, Food and Rural Affairs (DEFRA)
Tel.:   020 7238 3000
Address: Nobel House, 17 Smith Square, London, SW1P 3JR
Website: http://www.defra.gov.uk/

Name: Department of Transport, Local Government and Regions (DTLR)
Tel.:   020 7944 3000
Address: Eland House, Bressenden Place, London, SW1E 5DU
Website: http://www.dtlr.gov.uk/

Name: Department of Trade and Industry
Tel.:   020 7215 5000
Address: 1 Victoria Street, London SW1H 0ET
Website: http://www.dti.gov.uk/

Name: English Heritage
Tel.:   0870 333 1181
Address: Customer Services Department, PO Box 569, Swindon, SN2 2YP
Website: http://www.english-heritage.org.uk/

Name: English Nature
Tel.:   01733 455000
Address: Northminster House, Peterborough, PE1 1UA
Website: http://english-nature.org.uk/

Name: Environment Agency
Tel.:   01454 624400
Address: Head Office, Rio House, Waterside Drive, Aztec West, Almondsbury, Bristol, BS32 4UD
Website: http://www.environment-agency.gov.uk/

Name: Joint Nature Conservation Committee (JNCC)
Tel.:   01733 562626
Address: JNCC, Monkstone House, City Road, Peterborough, PE1 1JY
Website: http://www.jncc.gov.uk/

Name: Natural Environment Research Council (NERC)
Tel.:   01793 411500
Address: NERC, Polaris House, North Star Avenue, Swindon, SN2 1EU
Website: http://www.nerc.ac.uk/

Name: Office for National Statistics
Tel.:   0845 6013034
Address: The Library, Office for National Statistics, Cardiff Road, Newport, NP10 8XG
Website: http://www.statistics.gov.uk/

Name: Planning Inspectorate
Tel.:   0117 372 6372
Address: Temple Quay House, 2 The Square, Temple Quay, Bristol, BS1 6PN
Website: http://www.planninginspectorate.gov.uk/

Name: Royal Society for the Protection of Birds (RSPB)
Tel.:   01767 680551
Address: RSPB, The Lodge, Sandy, Bedfordshire, SG19 2DL
Website: http://www.rspb.org.uk/

Name: Scottish Natural Heritage
Tel.:   0131 447 4784
Address: Headquarters, 12 Hope Terrace, Edinburgh, EH9 2AS
Website: http://www.snh.org.uk/

Name: Scottish Environment Protection Agency (SEPA)
Tel.:   01786 457700
Address: SEPA Corporate Office, Erskine Court, Castle Business Park, Stirling, FK9 4TR
Website: http://www.sepa.org.uk/

Name: The Wildlife Trusts
Tel.:   01636 677711
Address: Headquarters, Mather Road, Newark, NG24 1WT
Website: http://www.wildlifetrusts.org/

Name: Wildfowl and Wetlands Trust
Tel.:   01453 891900
Address: Slimbridge, Gloucestershire, GL27 7BT
Website: http://www.wwt.org.uk/

Name: World Wide Fund for Nature (WWF)
Tel.:   01483 426444
Address: Panda House, Weyside Park, Godalming, Surrey, GU7 1XR
Website: http://www.wwf-uk.org/

The above list of key consultees and sources of information is not intended to be exhaustive. There are many other organizations and societies more specific to certain subject areas, concentrating on particular flora and fauna, for example, or certain aspects of built heritage or history. Other consultees and organizations will become 'key' depending upon the locality in question. Departments of local authorities will often be consultees, and Local Agenda 21 groups or local community groups are likely to be active and interested in spatially specific impacts.

Appendix 2

Projects to which the Town and Country Planning (Environmental Impact Assessment) (England and Wales) Regulations 1999 Apply: Schedule 2 Projects

1. In the table below:

    'area of the works' includes any area occupied by apparatus, equipment, machinery, materials, plant, spoil heaps or other facilities or stores required for construction or installation;
    'controlled waters' has the same meaning as in the Water Resources Act 1991[1];
    'floorspace' means the floorspace in a building or buildings.

2. The table below sets out the descriptions of development and applicable thresholds and criteria for the purpose of classifying development as Schedule 2 development.

[1] 1991 C. 57. *See* section 104.

Table

Column 1 Description of development	Column 2 Applicable thresholds and criteria	Column 3 Indicative thresholds and criteria

The carrying out of development to provide any of the following:

1. Agriculture and aquaculture

Column 1 Description of development	Column 2 Applicable thresholds and criteria	Column 3 Indicative thresholds and criteria
(a) Projects for the use of uncultivated land or semi-natural areas for intensive agricultural purposes;	The area of the development exceeds 0.5 hectare.	Development (such as greenhouses, farm buildings, etc.) on previously uncultivated land is unlikely to require EIA unless it covers more than 5 hectares. In considering whether particular development is likely to have significant effects, consideration should be given to impacts on the surrounding ecology, hydrology and landscape.
(b) Water management projects for agriculture, including irrigation and land drainage projects;	The area of the works exceeds 1 hectare.	EIA is more likely to be required if the development would result in permanent changes to the character of more than 5 hectares of land. In assessing the significance of any likely effects, particular regard should be had to whether the development would have damaging wider impacts on hydrology and surrounding ecosystems. It follows that EIA will not normally be required for routine water management projects undertaken by farmers.
(c) Intensive livestock installations (unless included in Schedule 1);	The area of new floorspace exceeds 500 square metres.	The significance or otherwise of the impacts of intensive livestock installations will often depend on the level of odours, increased traffic and the arrangements for waste handling. EIA is more likely to be required for intensive livestock installations if they are designed to house more than 750 sows, 2000 fattening pigs, 60 000 broilers or 50 000 layers, turkeys or other poultry.
(d) Intensive fish farming;	The installation resulting from the development is designed to produce more than 10 tonnes of dead weight fish per year.	Apart from the physical scale of any development, the likelihood of significant effects will generally depend on the extent of any likely wider impacts on the hydrology and ecology of the surrounding area. Developments designed to produce more than 100 tonnes (dead weight) of fish per year will be more likely to require EIA.
(e) Reclamation of land from the sea.	All development.	In assessing the significance of any development, regard should be had to the likely wider impacts on natural coastal processes beyond the site itself, as well as to the scale of reclamation works themselves. EIA is more likely to be required where work is proposed on a site which exceeds 1 hectare.

2. Extractive industry

Column 1 Description of development	Column 2 Applicable thresholds and criteria	Column 3 Indicative thresholds and criteria
(a) Quarries, open-cast mining and peat extraction (unless included in Schedule 1);	All development except the construction of buildings or other ancillary structures where the new floorspace does not exceed 1000 square metres.	The likelihood of significant effects will tend to depend on the scale and duration of the works, and the likely consequent impact of noise, dust, discharges to water and visual intrusion. All new open cast mines and underground mines will generally require EIA. For clay, sand and gravel workings, quarries and peat extraction sites, EIA is more likely to be required if they would cover more than 15 hectares or involve the extraction of more than 30 000 tonnes of mineral per year.
(b) Underground mining;		

Table (continued)

Column 1 Description of development	Column 2 Applicable thresholds and criteria	Column 3 Indicative thresholds and criteria
2. Extractive industry (continued)		
(c) Extraction of minerals by fluvial dredging;	All development.	Particular consideration should be given to noise, and any wider impacts on the surrounding hydrology and ecology. EIA is more likely to be required where it is expected that more than 100 000 tonnes of mineral will be extracted per year.
(d) Deep drillings, in particular: (i) geothermal drilling; (ii) drilling for the storage of nuclear waste material; (iii) drilling for water supplies; with the exception of drillings for investigating the stability of the soil.	(i) In relation to any type of drilling, the area of the works exceeds 1 hectare; or (ii) in relation to geothermal drilling and drilling for the storage of nuclear waste material, the drilling is within 100 metres of any controlled waters.	EIA is more likely to be required where the scale of the drilling operations involves development of a surface site of more than 5 hectares. Regard should be had to the likely wider impacts on surrounding hydrology and ecology. On its own, exploratory deep drilling is unlikely to require EIA. It would not be appropriate to require EIA for exploratory activity simply because it might eventually lead to some form of permanent activity.
(e) Surface industrial installations for the extraction of coal, petroleum, natural gas and ores, as well as bituminous shale.	The area of the development exceeds 0.5 hectare.	The main considerations are likely to be the scale of development, emissions to air, discharges to water, the risk of accident and the arrangements for transporting the fuel. EIA is more likely to be required if the development is on a major scale (site of 10 hectares or more) or where production is expected to be substantial (e.g. more than 100 000 tonnes of petroleum per year).
3. Energy industry		
(a) Industrial installations for the production of electricity, steam and hot water (unless included in Schedule 1);	The area of the development exceeds 0.5 hectare.	EIA will normally be required for power stations which require approval from the Secretary of State at the Department of Trade and Industry (i.e. those with a thermal output of more than 50 megawatts). EIA is unlikely to be required for smaller new conventional power stations. Small stations using novel forms of generation should be considered carefully in line with the guidance in PPG 22 (Renewable Energy). The main considerations are likely to be the level of emissions to air, arrangements for the transport of fuel and any visual impact.
(b) Industrial installations for carrying gas, steam and hot water;	The area of the works exceeds 1 hectare.	
(c) Surface storage of natural gas; (d) Underground storage of combustible gases; (e) Surface storage of fossil fuels;	(i) The area of any new building, deposit or structure exceeds 500 square metres; or (ii) a new building, deposit or structure is to be sited within 100 metres of any controlled waters.	In addition to the scale of the development, significant effects are likely to depend on discharges to water, emissions to air and risk to accidents. EIA is more likely to be required where it is proposed to store more than 100 000 tonnes of fuel. Smaller installations are unlikely to require EIA unless hazardous chemicals are stored.
(f) Industrial briquetting of coal and lignite;	The area of new floorspace exceeds 1000 square metres.	As paragraph 4 – Production and processing of metals.
(g) Installations for the processing and storage of radioactive waste (unless included in Schedule 1);	(i) The area of new floorspace exceeds 1000 square metres; or	EIA will normally be required for new installations whose primary purpose is to process and store radioactive waste, and which are located on sites not previously authorised for such use. In addition to the scale of any development, significant effects are likely to depend on the extent of routine

Table (continued)

Column 1 Description of development	Column 2 Applicable thresholds and criteria	Column 3 Indicative thresholds and criteria
3. Energy industry (continued)		
	(ii) the installation resulting from the development will require an authorisation or the variation of an authorisation under the Radioactive Substance Act 1993.	discharges of radiation to the environment. In this context EIA is unlikely to be required for installations where the processing or storage of radioactive waste is incidental to the main purpose of the development (e.g. installations at hospitals or research facilities).
(h) Installations for hydroelectric energy production;	The installation is designed to produce more than 0.5 megawatts.	In addition to the physical scale of the development, particular regard should be had to the potential wider impacts on hydrology and ecology. EIA is more likely to be required for new hydroelectric developments which have more than 5 megawatts of generating capacity.
(i) Installations for the harnessing of wind power for energy production (wind farms).	(i) The development involves the installation of more than 2 turbines; or (ii) the hub height of any turbine or height of any other structure exceeds 15 metres.	The likelihood of significant effects will generally depend on the scale of the development, and its visual impact, as well as potential noise impacts. EIA is more likely to be required for commercial developments of five or more turbines, or more than 5 megawatts of new generating capacity.
4. Production and processing of metals		

(a) Installations for the production of pig iron or steel (primary or secondary fusion) including continuous casting;
(b) Installations for the processing of ferrous metals:
  (i) hot-rolling mills;
  (ii) smitheries with hammers;
  (iii) application of protective fused metal coats;
	The area of new floorspace exceeds 1000 square metres.	New manufacturing or industrial plants of the types listed in the Regulations, may well require EIA if the operational development covers a site of more than 10 hectares. Smaller developments are more likely to require EIA if they are expected to give rise to significant discharges of waste, emission of pollutants or operational noise. Among the factors to be taken into account in assessing the significance of such effects are:
		
		• whether the development involves a process designated as a 'scheduled process' for the purpose of air pollution control;
		• whether the process involves discharges to water which require the consent of the Environment Agency;
		• whether the installation would give rise to the presence of environmentally significant quantities of potentially hazardous or polluting substances;
		• whether the process would give rise to radioactive or other hazardous waste;
		• whether the development would fall under Council Directive 96/82/EC on the control of major accident hazards involving dangerous substances (COMAH).
		
		However, the need for a consent under other legislation is not itself a justification for EIA.

(c) Ferrous metal foundries; (d) Installations for the smelting, including the alloyage, of non-ferrous metals, excluding precious metals, including recovered products (refining, foundry casting, etc.); (e) Installations for surface treatment of metals and plastic material using an electrolytic or chemical process; (f) Manufacture and assembly of motor vehicles and manufacture of motor-vehicle engines; (g) Shipyards; (h) Installations for the construction and repair of aircraft; (i) Manufacture of railway equipment; (j) Swaging by explosives; (k) Installations for the roasting and sintering of metallic ores.	The area of new floorspace exceeds 1000 square metres.	

Table (continued)

Column 1 Description of development	Column 2 Applicable thresholds and criteria	Column 3 Indicative thresholds and criteria
5. Mineral industry		
(a) Coke ovens (dry coal distillation); (b) Installations for the manufacture of cement; (c) Installations for the production of asbestos and the manufacture of asbestos-based products (unless included in Schedule 1); (d) Installations for the manufacture of glass including glass fibre; (e) Installations for smelting mineral substances including the production of mineral fibres; (f) Manufacture of ceramic products by burning, in particular roofing tiles, bricks, refractory bricks, tiles, stoneware or porcelain.	The area of new floorspace exceeds 1000 square metres.	As for paragraph 4.
6. Chemical industry (unless included in Schedule 1)		
(a) Treatment of intermediate products and production of chemicals; (b) Production of pesticides and pharmaceutical products paints and varnishes, elastomers and peroxides;	The area of new floorspace exceeds 1000 square metres.	
(c) Storage facilities for petroleum, petrochemical and chemical products.	(i) The area of any new building or structure exceeds 0.05 hectare; or (ii) more than 200 tonnes of petroleum, petrochemical or chemical products are to be stored at any one time	As for paragraph 4.
7. Food industry		
(a) Manufacture of vegetable and animal oils and fats; (b) Packing and canning of animal and vegetable products; (c) Manufacture of dairy products; (d) Brewing and malting; (e) Confectionery and syrup manufacture; (f) Installations for the slaughter of animals; (g) Industrial starch manufacturing installations; (h) Fish-meal and fish-oil factories; (i) Sugar factories.	The area of new floorspace exceeds 1000 square metres.	As for paragraph 4.

Table (continued)

Column 1 Description of development	Column 2 Applicable thresholds and criteria	Column 3 Indicative thresholds and criteria
8. Textile, leather, wood and paper industries		
(a) Industrial plants for the production of paper and board (unless included in Schedule 1); (b) Plants for the pre-treatment (operations such as washing, bleaching, mercerisation) or dyeing of fibres or textiles; (c) Plants for the tanning of hides and skins; (d) Cellulose-processing and production installations.	The area of new floorspace exceeds 1000 square metres.	As for paragraph 4.
9. Rubber industry		
Manufacture and treatment of elastomer-based products.	The area of new floorspace exceeds 1000 square metres.	As for paragraph 4.
10. Infrastructure projects		
(a) Industrial estate development projects;	The area of the development exceeds 0.5 hectare.	EIA is more likely to be required if the site area of the new development is more than 20 hectares. In determining whether significant effects are likely, particularly consideration should be given to the potential increase in traffic, emissions and noise.
(b) Urban development projects, including the construction of shopping centres and car parks, sports stadiums, leisure centres and multiplex cinemas;	The area of the development exceeds 0.5 hectare.	In addition to the physical scale of such developments, particular consideration should be given to the potential increase in traffic, emissions and noise. EIA is unlikely to be required for the redevelopment of land unless the new development is on a significantly greater scale than the previous use, or the types of impact are of a markedly different nature or there is a high level of contamination. Development proposed for sites which have not previously been intensively developed are more likely to require EIA if: • the site area of the scheme is more than 5 hectares; or • it would provide a total of more than 10 000 square metres of new commercial floorspace; or • the development would have significant urbanising effects in a previously non-urbanised area (e.g. a new development of more than 1000 dwellings).
(c) Construction of intermodal transshipment facilities and of intermodal terminals (unless included in Schedule 1);	The area of the development exceeds 0.5 hectare.	In addition to the physical scale of the development, particular impacts for consideration are increased traffic, noise, emissions to air and water. Developments of more than 5 hectares are more likely to require EIA.
(d) Construction of railways (unless included in Schedule 1);	The area of the works exceeds 1 hectare.	For linear transport schemes, the likelihood of significant effects will generally depend on the estimated emissions, traffic, noise and vibration and degree of visual intrusion and impact on the

Table (continued)

Column 1 Description of development	Column 2 Applicable thresholds and criteria	Column 3 Indicative thresholds and criteria
10. Infrastructure projects (continued)		
		surrounding ecology. EIA is more likely to be required for new development over 2 kilometres in length.
(e) Construction of airfields (unless included in Schedule 1);	(i) The development involves an extension to a runway; or (ii) the area of the works exceeds 1 hectare.	The main impacts to be considered in judging significance are noise, traffic generation and emissions. New permanent airfields will normally require EIA, as will major works (such as new runways or terminals with a site area of more than 10 hectares) at existing airports. Smaller scale development at existing airports is unlikely to require EIA unless it would lead to significant increases in air or road traffic.
(f) Construction of roads (unless included in Schedule 1);	The area of the works exceeds 1 hectare.	As for paragraph 10(d).
(g) Construction of harbours and port installations including fishing harbours (unless included in Schedule 1);	The area of the works exceeds 1 hectare.	Primary impacts for consideration are those on hydrology, ecology, noise and increased traffic. EIA is more likely to be required if the development is on a major scale (e.g. would cover a site of more than 10 hectares). Smaller developments may also have significant effects where they include a quay or pier which would extend beyond the high water mark or would affect wider coastal processes.
(h) Inland-waterway construction not included in Schedule 1, canalisation and flood-relief works;	The area of the works exceeds 1 hectare.	The likelihood of significant impacts is likely to depend primarily on the potential wider impacts on the surrounding hydrology and ecology. EIA is more likely to be required for development of over 2 kilometres of canal. The impact of flood relief works is especially dependent on the nature of the location and the potential effects on the surrounding ecology and hydrology. Schemes for which the area of the works would exceed 5 hectares or which are more than 2 kilometres in length would normally require EIA.
(i) Dams and other installations designed to hold water or store it on a long-term basis (unless included in Schedule 1);	The area of the works exceeds 1 hectare.	In considering such developments, particular regard should be had to the potential wider impacts on the hydrology and ecology, as well as to the physical scale of the development. EIA is likely to be required for any major new dam (e.g. where the construction site exceeds 20 hectares).
(j) Tramways, elevated and underground railways, suspended lines or similar lines of a particular type, used exclusively or mainly for passenger transport;	The area of the works exceeds 1 hectare.	As for paragraph 10(d).
(k) Oil and gas pipe-line installations (unless included in Schedule 1);	(i) The area of the works exceeds 1 hectare; or, (ii) In the case of a gas pipe-line, the installation has a design operating pressure exceeding 7 bar gauge.	For underground pipe-lines, the major impact to be considered will generally be the disruption to the surrounding ecosystems during construction, while for overground pipe-lines visual impact will be a key consideration. EIA is more likely to be required for any pipe-line over 5 kilometres long. EIA is

Table (continued)

Column 1 Description of development	Column 2 Applicable thresholds and criteria	Column 3 Indicative thresholds and criteria
10. Infrastructure projects (continued)		
(l) Installations of long-distance aqueducts;		unlikely to be required for pipe-lines laid underneath a road, or for those installed entirely by means of tunnelling.
(m) Coastal work to combat erosion and maritime works capable of altering the coast through the construction, for example, of dykes, moles, jetties and other sea defence works, excluding the maintenance and reconstruction of such works;	All development.	The impact of such works will depend largely on the nature of the particular site and the likely wider impacts on natural coastal processes outside the site. EIA will be more likely where the area of the works would exceed 1 hectare.
(n) Groundwater abstraction and artificial groundwater recharge schemes not included in Schedule 1; (o) Works for the transfer of water resources between river basins not included in Schedule 1;	The area of the works exceeds 1 hectare.	Impacts likely to be significant are those on hydrology and ecology. Developments of this sort can have significant effects on environments some kilometres distant. This is particularly important for wetland and other sites where the habitat and species are particularly dependent on an aquatic environment. EIA is likely to be required for developments where the area of the works exceeds 1 hectare.
(p) Motorway service areas.	The area of the development exceeds 0.5 hectare.	Impacts likely to be significant for traffic, noise, air quality, ecology and visual impact. EIA is more likely to be required for new motorway service areas which are proposed for previously undeveloped sites and if the proposed development would cover an area of more than 5 hectares.
11. Other projects		
(a) Permanent racing and test tracks for motorised vehicles;	The area of the development exceeds 1 hectare.	Particular consideration should be given to the size, noise impacts, emissions and the potential traffic generation. EIA is more likely to be required for developments with a site area of 20 hectares or more.
(b) Installations for the disposal of waste (unless included in Schedule 1);	(i) The disposal is by incineration; or (ii) the area of the development exceeds 0.5 hectare; or (iii) the installation is to be sited within 100 metres of any controlled waters.	The likelihood of significant effects will generally depend on the scale of the development and the nature of the potential impact in terms of discharge, emissions or odour. For installations (including landfill sites) for the deposit, recovery and/or disposal of household, industrial and/or commercial wastes (as defined by the Controlled Waste Regulations 1992) EIA is more likely to be required where new capacity is created to hold more than 50 000 tonnes per year, or to hold waste on a site of 10 hectares or more. Sites taking smaller quantities of these wastes, sites seeking only to accept inert wastes (demolition rubble, etc.) or civic amenity sites, are unlikely to require EIA.
(c) Waste water treatment plants (unless included in Schedule 1);	The area of the development exceeds 1000 square metres.	Particular consideration should be given to the size, treatment process, pollution and nuisance potential, topography, proximity of dwellings and the

Table (continued)

Column 1 Description of development	Column 2 Applicable thresholds and criteria	Column 3 Indicative thresholds and criteria
11. Other projects (continued)		
		potential impact of traffic movements. EIA is more likely to be required if the development would be on a substantial scale (e.g. site area of more than 10 hectares) or if it would lead to significant discharges (e.g. capacity exceeding 100 000 population equivalent). EIA should not be required simply because a plant is on a scale which required compliance with the Urban Waste Water Treatment Directive (91/271/EEC).
(d) Sludge-deposition site;	(i) The area of deposit or storage exceeds 0.5 hectare; or (ii) a deposit is to be made or scrap stored within 100 metres of any controlled waters.	Similar considerations will apply for sewage sludge lagoons as for waste disposal installations. EIA is more likely to be required where the site is intended to hold more than 5000 cubic metres of sewage sludge.
(e) Storage of scrap iron, including scrap vehicles;		Major impacts from storage of scrap iron are likely to be discharges to soil, site noise and traffic generation. EIA is more likely to be required where it is proposed to store scrap on an area of 10 hectares or more.
(f) Test benches for engines, turbines or reactors; (g) Installations for the manufacture of artificial mineral fibres; (h) Installations for the recovery or destruction of explosive substances; (i) Knackers' yards.	The area of new floorspace exceeds 1000 square metres.	As for paragraph 4.
12. Tourism and leisure		
(a) Ski-runs, ski-lifts and cable-cars and associated developments;	(i) The area of the works exceeds 1 hectare; or (ii) the height of any building or other structure exceeds 15 metres.	EIA is more likely to be required if the development is over 500 metres in length or if it requires a site of more than 5 hectares. In addition to any visual or ecological impacts, particular regard should also be had to the potential traffic generation.
(b) Marinas;	The area of the enclosed water surface exceeds 1000 square metres.	In assessing whether significant effects are likely, particular regard should be had to any wider impacts on natural coastal processes outside the site, as well as the potential noise and traffic generation. EIA is more likely to be required for large new marinas, for example where the proposal is for more than 300 berths (seawater site) or 100 berths (freshwater site). EIA is unlikely to be required where the development is located solely within an existing dock or basin.
(c) Holiday villages and hotel complexes outside urban areas and associated developments; (d) Theme parks;	The area of the development exceeds 0.5 hectare.	In assessing the significance of tourism development, visual impacts, impacts on ecosystems and traffic generation will be key considerations. The effects of new theme parks are more likely to be significant if it is expected that they will generate more than 250 000 visitors per year. EIA is likely to be required for major new tourism and leisure
(e) Permanent camp sites and caravan sites;	The area of the development exceeds 1 hectare.	

Table (continued)

Column 1 Description of development	Column 2 Applicable thresholds and criteria	Column 3 Indicative thresholds and criteria
12. Tourism and leisure (continued)		
		developments which require a site of more than 10 hectares. In particular, EIA is more likely to be required for holiday villages or hotel complexes with more than 300 bed spaces, or for permanent camp sites or caravan sites with more than 200 pitches.
(f) Golf courses and associated developments.	The area of the development exceeds 1 hectare.	New 18-hole golf courses are likely to require EIA. The main impacts are likely to be those on the surrounding hydrology, ecosystems and landscape, as well as those from traffic generation. Developments at existing golf courses are unlikely to require EIA.
13.		
(a) Any change to or extension of development of a description listed in Schedule 1 or in paragraphs 1 to 12 of Column 1 of this table, where that development is already authorised, executed or in the process of being executed, and the change or extension may have significant adverse effects on the environment;	(i) In relation to development of a description mentioned in Column 1 of this table, the thresholds and criteria in the corresponding part of Column 2 of this table applied to the change or extension (and not to the development as changed or extended). (ii) In relation to development of a description mentioned in a paragraph in Schedule 1 (see Appendix 1) indicated below, the thresholds and criteria in Column 2 of the paragraph of this table indicated below applied to the change or extension (and not to the development as changed or extended):	Development which comprises a change or extension requires EIA only if the change or extension is likely to have significant environmental effects. This should be considered in the light of the general guidance in DETR Circular 2/99 (Welsh Office Circular 11/99) and the indicative thresholds shown above in Column 3. However, the significance of any effects must be considered in the context of the existing development. In some cases, repeated small extensions may be made to development. Quantified thresholds cannot easily deal with this kind of 'incremental' development. In such instances, it should be borne in mind that the Column 3 thresholds are indicative only. An expansion of the same size as a previous expansion will not automatically lead to the same determination on the need for EIA because the environment may have altered since the question was last addressed.

Paragraph in Schedule 1	Paragraph of this table
1	6(a)
2(a)	3(a)
2(b)	3(g)
3	3(g)
4	4
5	5
6	6(a)
7(a)	10(d) (in relation to railways) or 10(e) (in relation to airports)
7(b) and (c)	10(f)
8(a)	10(h)
8(b)	10(g)
9	11(b)
10	11(b)
11	10(n)

Table (continued)

Column 1 Description of development	Column 2 Applicable thresholds and criteria		Column 3 Indicative thresholds and criteria
13. (continued)			
	12	10(o)	
	13	11(c)	
	14	2(e)	
	15	10(i)	
	16	10(k)	
	17	1(c)	
	18	8(a)	
	19	2(a)	
	20	6(c).	
(b) Development of a description mentioned in Schedule 1 undertaken exclusively or mainly for the development and testing of new methods or products and not used for more than two years.	All development.		

Appendix 3

Schedule 4: Requirements of the Regulations as to the Content of Environmental Statements

Below are the statutory provisions with respect to the content of environmental statements, as set out in Parts I and II of Schedule 4 to the Town and Country Planning (Environmental Impact Assessment) (England and Wales) Regulations 1999.

Under the definition in Regulation 2(1), 'environmental statement' means a statement:

(a) that includes such of the information referred to in Part I of Schedule 4 as is reasonably required to assess the environmental effects of the development and which the applicant can, having regard in particular to current knowledge and methods of assessment, reasonably be required to compile, but

(b) that includes at least the information referred to in Part II of Schedule 4.

Part I

1. Description of the development, including in particular:

    (a) a description of the physical characteristics of the whole development and the land-use requirements during the construction and operational phases;

    (b) a description of the main characteristics of the production process, for instance, nature and quantity of the materials used;

    (c) an estimate, by type and quantity, of expected residues and emissions (water, air and soil pollution, noise, vibration, light, heat, radiation, etc.) resulting from the operation of the proposed development.

2. An outline of the main alternatives studied by the applicant or appellant and an indication of the main reasons for his choice, taking into account the environmental effects.

3. A description of the aspects of the environment likely to be significantly affected by the development, including, in particular, population, fauna, flora, soil, water, air, climatic factors, material assets, including the architectural and archaeological heritage, landscape and the inter-relationship between the above factors.

4. A description of the likely significant effects of the development on the environment, which should cover the direct effects and any indirect, secondary, cumulative, short, medium and long-term, permanent and temporary, positive and negative effects of the development, resulting from:

    (a) the existence of the development;

    (b) the use of natural resources;

    (c) the emission of pollutants, the creation of nuisances and the elimination of waste,

    and the description by the applicant of the forecasting methods used to assess the effects on the environment.

5. A description of the measures envisaged to prevent, reduce and where possible offset any significant adverse effects on the environment.

6. A non-technical summary of the information provided under paragraphs 1 to 5 of this Part.

7. An indication of any difficulties (technical deficiencies or lack of know-how) encountered by the applicant in compiling the required information.

Part II

1. A description of the development comprising information on the site, design and size of the development.

2. A description of the measures envisaged in order to avoid, reduce and, if possible, remedy significant adverse effects.

3. The data required to identify and assess the main effects which the development is likely to have on the environment.

4. An outline of the main alternatives studied by the applicant or appellant and an indication of the main reasons for his choice, taking into account the environmental effects.

5. A non-technical summary of the information provided under paragraphs 1 to 4 of this Part.

Appendix 4

Review Criteria

The following identifies those criteria commonly used by reviewers of the content and quality of Environmental Statements (ESs).

General

Scoping

- Description of the scoping process
- Consultation record – consultees and responses
- Reasons for exclusion of issues.

Alternatives

- Locations, construction and operational processes, site layouts
- Analysis of advantages and disadvantages of each option
- Description of reasons for selection
- Description of other factors influencing the final choice.

Description of the Proposed Development

- Purpose and objectives
- Programme for construction, operation, decommissioning and restoration
- Methods of construction
- Physical characteristics – location, design, size, area of land take
- Nature and quantity of materials
- Type and quantity of traffic
- Type and quantity of emissions and residues.

Site Description

- Existing land use of site and surrounding area
- Description of plans, policies and designations of site and surroundings.

Topic Specific

These criteria are tested for each topic, e.g. noise, water. Where appropriate, impacts evaluated should include direct, indirect, cumulative, short, medium and long term, permanent and temporary, positive and negative, reversible and irreversible.

Baseline Conditions

- Description of current condition
- Source of data

- Evaluation of sensitivity and importance
- Limitations of surveys.

Prediction of Impact Magnitude

- Predictions of the magnitude of likely significant effects
- Predictions for each phase of development
- Methods of prediction should be described
- Levels of confidence should be described.

Impact Significance

- Description of standards, thresholds and limits
- Identify significance of impacts after mitigation.

Mitigation

- Measures to avoid, reduce or remedy adverse impacts
- Statement of effectiveness of mitigation
- Commitment to mitigation.

Post-development

- Management plans
- Monitoring.

Presentation of Results

Presentation

- Clear and logical
- Avoid technical terms; use of glossary
- Provision of references
- Provision of plans, figures, illustrations.

Objectivity

- Balanced and unbiased
- Summary of issues raised by consultees
- Identification of difficulties in assessment.

Non-technical Summary

- Information for non-specialist to understand environmental effects of development
- Summary of description of development, alternatives, aspects of environment likely to be significantly affected, significant impacts, mitigation measures
- Provision as a stand alone document with appropriate maps and illustrations
- Accurate reflection of ES findings.

Review Grades

A   Excellent, no tasks left incomplete.
B   Good, only minor omissions and inadequacies.
C   Satisfactory despite omissions and inadequacies.
D   Parts well attempted, but must as a whole be considered unsatisfactory because of omissions and/or inadequacies.
E   Poor, significant omissions or inadequacies.
F   Very poor, most tasks left incomplete.
N/A   Not applicable. The review topic is not applicable or relevant in the context of this statement.

Source: Adapted from IEMA Review Criteria and Lee and Colley 1990.

Appendix 5

Bibliography and References

These are some of the main texts giving guidance on various techniques and methods of EIA. Attention is drawn to more specific sources of information in the relevant sections of the book.

British Medical Association 1999. *Health and Environmental Impact Assessment – An Integrated Approach*. Earthscan Publications Ltd.

Byron, H. 2000. *Biodiversity and EIA: A Good Practice Guide for Road Schemes*. RSPB *et al.*, London.

Construction Industry Research and Information Association 1994. *Environmental Assessment*. CIRIA.

Construction Industry Research and Information Association 2000. *Sustainable Urban Drainage Systems*. CIRIA C522, London.

Countryside Agency *et al.* 2001. *Quality of Life Capital*. Countryside Agency, Cheltenham.

Countryside Commission 1993. *Landscape Character Assessment Guidelines*. CCP 423. Countryside Commission, Cheltenham.

Countryside Commission 1994. *Design in the Countryside*. CCP 418. Countryside Commission, Cheltenham.

Department of Environment 1995. *Preparation of Environmental Statements for Planning Projects That Require Environmental Assessment – A Good Practice Guide*. HMSO, London.

Department of Environment, Transport and the Regions 1997. *Mitigation Measures Used in Environmental Statements*. HMSO, London.

Department of Environment, Transport and the Regions 1999. *Environmental Impact Assessment*. Circular 02/99. HMSO, London.

Department of Environment, Transport and the Regions 2000. *Environmental Impact Assessment – A Guide to Procedures*. Thomas Telford Ltd, London.

Earll, R. (on behalf of Joint Nature Conservation Committee and Marine Conservation Society) 1992. *The SEASEARCH Habitat Guide – An Identification Guide to the Main Habitats Found in the Shallow Seas around the British Isles*. Marine Conservation Society, Ross on Wye.

Environment Agency 1996. *Environmental Assessment: Scoping Handbook for Projects*. Environment Agency, Bristol.

European Commission 2001. *Guidance on Screening and Scoping*. Brussels.

Glasson, J., Therivel, R. and Chadwick, A. 1999. *Introduction to Environmental Impact Assessment*, second edition. UCL Press.

Goodland, R. and Sadler, B. 1996. The analysis of environmental sustainability from concepts to application. *International Journal of Sustainable Development*.

Harrop, O. and Nixon, A. 1999. *Environmental Assessment in Practice*. Routledge, London.

Institute of Environmental Assessment 1993. Guidelines for the environmental assessment of road traffic. IEA, Lincoln.

Institution of Highways and Transportation 1994. Guidelines for Traffic Impact Assessment. IHT, London.

Institute of Environmental Assessment 1995. *Guidelines for Baseline Ecological Assessment*. E & FN Spon, London.

Institute of Environmental Assessment and Landscape Institute 1995. *Guidelines for Landscape and Visual Impact Assessment*. E & FN Spon, London.

Joint Nature Conservation Committee (JNCC) 1990. *Handbook for Phase I Habitat Survey – A Technique for Environmental Audit*. JNCC, London.

Kent County Council (Planning Department) 1991. *Environmental Assessment Hand Book*. Kent County Council, Maidstone.

Morris, P. and Therivel, R. 2001. *Methods of Environmental Impact Assessment*, second edition. E. & F.N. Spon, London.

Petts, J. 1999. *Handbook of Environmental Impact Assessment*, Vols 1 and 2. Blackwell Science, Oxford.

Ratcliffe, D.A. 1977. *A Nature Conservation Review*. Cambridge University Press, Cambridge.

Singleton, R. *et al.* 1999. *Environmental Assessment*. Thomas Telford Ltd, London.

Treweek, J. 1999. *Ecological Impact Assessment*. Blackwell Science.

Wathern, P. (ed.) 1992. *Environmental Impact Assessment: Theory and Practice*, second edition. Routledge, London.

Weston, J. 1997. *Planning and Environmental Impact Assessment in Practice*. Longman, Harlow.

Wood, C. 2002. *Environmental Impact Assessment – a Comparative Review*, second edition. Longman Scientific & Technical, Harlow.

World Bank 1996. *Environmental Assessment Source Book*. World Bank. Washington, DC.

Appendix 6

Organizations

Key Professional Organizations

Name:	Chartered Institute of Environmental Health (CIEH)
Tel.:	020 7928 6006
Address:	Chadwick Court, 15 Hatfields, London, SE1 8DJ
Website:	http://www.cieh.org.uk

Name:	Chartered Institute of Wastes Management (IWM)
Tel.:	01604 620426
Address:	9 Saxon Court, St Peter's Gardens, Northampton, NN1 1SX
Website:	http://www.iwm.co.uk

Name:	Chartered Institution of Water and Environmental Management (CIWEM)
Tel.:	020 7831 3110
Address:	15 John Street, London, WC1N 2EB
Website:	http://www.ciwem.org.uk

Name:	Chartered Landscape Institute (CLI)
Tel.:	020 7350 5200
Address:	The Landscape Institute, 6–8 Barnard Mews, London, SW11 1QU
Website:	http://www.l-i.org.uk

Name:	Institution of Civil Engineers
Tel.:	020 7222 7722
Address:	1 Great George Street, Westminster, London, SW1P 3AA
Website:	http://www.ice.org.uk

Name:	Institute of Ecology and Environmental Management (IEEM)
Tel.:	01962 868626
Address:	45 Southgate Street, Winchester, Hants, SO23 9EH
Website:	http://www.ieem.org.uk

Name:	Institute of Environmental Management and Assessment (IEMA)
Tel.:	01522 540069
Address:	St Nicholas House, 70 Newport, Lincoln, LN1 3DP
Website:	http://www.iema.net

Name:	Institute of Field Archaeologists (IFA)
Tel.:	0118 931 6446
Address:	IFA, University of Reading, 2 Earley Gate, PO Box 239, Reading, RG6 6AU
Website:	http://www.archaeologists.net

Name:	Institute of Leisure and Amenity Management (ILAM)
Tel.:	01491 874800
Address:	ILAM House, Lower Basildon, Reading, RG8 9NE
Website:	http://www.ilam.co.uk

Name:	International Association for Impact Assessment (IAIA)
Tel.:	+1 701 797 7908
Address:	IAIA Executive Office, 1330 23rd Street South, Suite C, Fargo, ND 58103, USA
Website:	http://www.iaia.org

Name:	National Society for Clean Air and Environmental Protection (NSCA)
Tel.:	01273 878770
Address:	44 Grand Parade, Brighton, BN2 2QA
Website:	http://www.nsca.org.uk

Name:	Royal Town Planning Institute (RTPI)
Tel.:	020 7636 9107
Address:	26 Portland Square, London W1N 4BE
Website:	http://www.rtpi.org.uk

Appendix 7

Training Courses

Useful Courses

The courses listed here are a sample of those which focus specifically on EIA. There are also numerous courses in the environmental planning and management fields which include EIA as a component. Advice on the suitability of courses can be sought from IEMA.

University of Bath
MSc/PGDip Integrated Environmental Management
Part Time Distance Learning (International)
http://www.bath.ac.uk

Oxford Brookes University
MSc/Dip Environmental Assessment and Management
MSc Planning and Environmental Assessment
MSc GIS and Environmental Assessment
Full Time/Part Time
http://www.brookes.ac.uk

University of Manchester
MA Environmental Impact Assessment and Management
Full Time
http://www.art.man.ac.uk

University of Aberystwyth
MSc/Dip in Environmental Impact Assessment
Full Time Distance Learning and International
http://www.aber.ac.uk

University of Brighton
MSc Environmental Assessment
Full Time/Part Time
http://www.brighton.ac.uk

University of East Anglia
MSc in EIA, Auditing and Management Systems
Full Time/Part Time/Distance Learning
http://www.uea.ac.uk

London School of Economics
MSc Environmental Assessment and Evaluation
Full Time/Part Time
http://www.lse.ac.uk

Wye College
PGDip Environmental Assessment and Management
Full Time
http://www.wye.ac.uk

Farnborough College of Technology
MSc Environmental Management
Full Time, Part Time
http://www.farn-ct.ac.uk

Short Training Courses

Oxford Brookes University

'The Impacts Assessment Unit has a well established and successful programme of one-day training courses on EIA and related areas. These courses, aimed primarily at local authorities and environmental consultancies, can be tailored to the specific requirements of individual clients. Our current programme includes the following:

- Introduction to EIA
- Methods of EIA
- Current Issues In EIA
- Environmental Law and Planning
- Environmental Appraisal of Development Plans
- Environmental Risk Assessment and Management
- Dealing With Contaminated Land'

http://www.brookes.ac.uk

Manchester University

'The EIA Centre organizes open conferences, seminars and courses of varying duration on various EIA themes. In addition, it has organized training courses for particular organizations (e.g. Environment Agency, English Nature and Cheshire County Council) and expects to continue this type of work in the future. It also participates, with other training institutions, in providing EIA training elsewhere in the UK, in developing countries, in the transitional countries of Central and Eastern Europe, and in other overseas countries. Opportunities exist at the Centre to undertake specially designed programmes of EIA study and training of varying duration.'

http://www.art.man.ac.uk

Index